We all know that highly intelligent people are not always loveable. Moreover, since stupidity and turpitude are, alas, by no means mutually exclusive, we are glad to find *either* quality: loveability *or* intelligence.

When, however, we do find high intelligence combined with notable rectitude and a truly loving heart, the result is irresistible.

Such are the very real people in this book. They are all apostles of a divine wisdom—they are *apostles extraordinary*.

Other books by Geddes MacGregor

APOSTLES EXTRAORDINARY

A Celebration of Saints and Sinners

Geddes MacGregor

Strawberry Hill Press

Strawberry Hill Press
2594 15th Avenue
San Francisco, California 94127

Edited and wordprocessed by Joseph Lubow
Typeset by Cragmont/Ex-Press, Oakland, California
Cover and book design by Ku, Fu-sheng
Proofread by Candace Judd
Printed by Edwards Brothers, Inc., Ann Arbor, Michigan

Manufactured in the United States of America

The chapter entitled "Duncan MacGregor" is based on articles contributed by the author to *The Aberdeen University Review* (XLIX, 2, Autumn, 1981) and *The Scots Magazine* (February, 1982), to both of which grateful acknowledgment is made.

Library of Congress Cataloging-in-Publication Data
MacGregor, Geddes.
    Apostles extraordinary

    Includes bibliographies and index
    1. Christian biography. I. Title.
BR1700.2.M28   1986   280'.092'2 [B]   85-22118
ISBN 0-89407-065-7 (pbk.)

To
Allan W. Campbell

Table of Contents

PREFACE

We all know that highly intelligent people are not always lovable. Moreover, since stupidity and turpitude are, alas, by no means mutually exclusive, we are glad to find *either* quality: lovability *or* intelligence. When, however, we do find high intelligence combined with notable rectitude and a truly loving heart, the result is irresistible. Such are the very real people in this book. They are all, each in his or her own very special way, apostles of a divine wisdom beyond the words of all the religions of the world yet accessible to loving hearts everywhere: apostles extraordinary.

An apostle (*apostolos*, a messenger or envoy) has a commission, the limits of which are usually defined. The apostolate I celebrate in this book has, however, no bounds; nor have these apostles any such limited commission as do ambassadors and consuls and envoys plenipotentiary. They are in the diplomatic service of wisdom and love: apostles extraordinary.

That I have had the good fortune to have known so well the eleven I describe is what Charles Williams would have called "holy luck." All are deceased, qualifying them for my private canonization. Most, though not all, are Victorian by birth and, in the words of the writer of Ecclesiasticus, have "won fame in their own generation." Each is unique. In the last chapter I record encounters with others I have known less well and in some cases have only casually met. When I tell students today that in my youth I met Kipling and Chesterton together at a luncheon in London, they tend to eye me with as much astonishment, not to say incredulity, as if I had said Shakespeare and Milton. I hope such younger people will welcome first-hand impressions of great men and women from a now bygone age. I know that many older people will find in them not merely nostalgic delight but encouragement and hope for the unfolding of a better world than is generally reflected in the daily news. I have tried to be not merely hagiographical but to show my characters, "warts and all." Nothing, however, can disguise my admiration or conceal my love.

Geddes MacGregor

ONE

John Gray

The mysterious figure of John Henry Gray (1866-1934) has become, in recent years, the center of a literary cult. In the late twenties and early thirties to which the following account belongs, he was little known beyond a small, not to say esoteric, circle; nor did he wish otherwise. He was by then well established as a Roman Catholic priest in charge of a parish in Edinburgh, Scotland, at a time when and in a place where his remarkable past could be well hid. His distinctive personality, however, expressed in his priestly ministrations, was strikingly unusual.

Of humble origin (of which by then every trace had been erased), he had been born and bred in London. His father was of Scottish descent: a carpenter and wheelwright at the Woolwich dockyard. The family was nonconformist, possibly Methodist. John was one of nine children.

The family's modest circumstances forced him to leave school at thirteen to work as a metal turner. In 1884, he passed a civil service examination that got him employment in the Lost Letters department of the London General Post Office. He educated himself to the point of passing the London University Matriculation and then obtaining a position in the Library of the Foreign Office: no easy achievement in those days for a lad of his background.

Soon he was making his way into the rarefied atmosphere of literary circles that included writers such as Pierre Louÿs and Oscar Wilde. Sometime after the arrest and imprisonment of Wilde on a homosexual charge, Gray, who had become a Roman Catholic, went to Rome to study for the priesthood. By this time he had formed a very close friendship with the son of a rich Russian Jewish family of international bankers in Paris, who remained deeply devoted to him until only death separated them and who liberally supported him throughout his priestly life, virtually building for him the beautiful church that was the focus of his ministry.

The author's recollections of Gray in the last decade of his life show him as the strangely fascinating figure that he was: an echo of an even then long bygone late Victorian age, yet imprinting himself with no uncertainty on the age in which he lived as a faithful priest in a quiet corner of a northern capital, infinitely remote from the scenes of his youth.

Yours ever, Dorian
—Letter to Oscar Wilde

No one even slightly knowledgeable in architecture and even vaguely interested in ecclesiastical by-ways could fail to be impressed by a little church in Edinburgh dedicated to St. Peter the Apostle. Designed by the most eminent Scottish architect of his time, Robert Lorimer, this uniquely charming church, impeccably tasteful inside and out looks like a little early Christian church in Italy. It stands at the corner of Falcon Avenue where it meets Falcon Gardens in the self-consciously respectable and somewhat heavily stonebuilt middle class district of Morningside. The church, whose smiling *cortile* seems mysteriously sunlit even on one of Edinburgh's darker days, appears like a solitary *Edelweiss* in full bloom piercing the dour stoniness of all around it. It is almost as unlikely there as would be a Rhine castle in Sicily or Greece. And if it be paradoxical today, it must have seemed even more so on that spring day in 1907 when it was blessed by the Archbishop in whose presence was sung High Mass, for in those Edwardian days Edinburgh was even more staid and more sternly hostile to Catholic influence than she is today.

When I first visited the church in 1926, at the age of sixteen, the aroma of incense that exuded from it as one opened the great soft-closing leather-covered doors seemed to have been wafted across a thousand years of prayer. I stood inside, transfixed at the simple beauty: the reredos of white and green marble, quarried in Greece, the coffered roof of Oregon pine supported by high piers, the painting by Sir Frank Brangwyn, richly framed behind the high altar and depicting Peter confessing his faith, and the striking rood with anchor-shaped base hanging from the sanctuary arch, all in sharp contrast to the chaste, dignified simplicity of the brick and whitewashed walls.[1] Yet the exquisite tastefulness of the furnishings paled before the striking figure of the celebrant making his way down the nave in a rich cope, stepping briskly a pace ahead of the other ministers on either side of him as he performed the rite of the *Asperges* before High Mass.

The paradoxes attending the presence of that Catholic corner of Edinburgh were the merest outward vesture of those attending the superlatively dignified and enigmatic incumbent, the Reverend Father John Gray who, with the liberal financial assistance of a Paris-born Russian Jewish convert to the Catholic faith, Marc-André Raffalovich, had built the church. Raffalovich (nicknamed Raffy) was the son of a rich international banker and of a mother whose Paris *salon* at 19 avenue Hoche had been the scene of a brilliant circle including Henri Bergson, Lanfrey, Sarah Bernhardt, and Ernest Renan, and who had been a close friend of the eminent French physiologist, Claude Bernard. In 1905, about the time the church was being built, Raffalovich decided to come to Edinburgh so as to be near his old and treasured friend John Gray, and acquired a large house at 9 Whitehouse Terrace within walking distance of St. Peter's. When André, as he preferred his friends to call him, died in 1934, the house was bought by John Baillie, a well-known Presbyterian divine and later Moderator of the General Assembly of the Kirk who had then just returned from America to his native Scotland. Paradox seemed to haunt everything that came even indirectly within the ambit of the unique personality of John Gray.

I met Father Gray in my teens because I had stumbled on his church at a time when I was fascinated by Roman Catholicism. So far I had encountered none but the most blatantly anti-intellectual priests. He seemed to breathe an atmosphere such as I somehow expected, but hitherto had never found, in the venerable tradition of christianized *romanitas*. I had not the slightest inkling of a suspicion that he had been, in his youth, a member of Oscar Wilde's circle in London, or that he had renounced his life there in the *fin de siècle*, exchanging it eventually for the disciplined life of a faithful parish priest in the Scottish capital. Nor would it have meant much to me at the time had I been told of it, for like many others of my age and circumstances I was notably ignorant of matters such as had brought notoriety and disgrace to Wilde a generation earlier. I saw in Father Gray only a delightfully cultivated man, an obviously dedicated parish priest with a punctiliousness in the performance of his duties such as one would more readily associate with an exceptionally well-trained English army officer rather than with a Roman Catholic priest in Scotland.

Both his manner and his facial expression reflected an enigmatic aloofness that pervaded all he said and did. His reddish complexion and high cheekbones somehow intensified the aloofness of his glance and adorned the striking dignity of his bearing. Yet what precisely gave him so striking a personality was by no means easily detected. From the accounts of those who knew him better than I ever did, his reticence and restraint were masks disguising a warm nature, but to that warmth I never penetrated. What came across to me was a studied politeness along with the kind of rigidity of formal devotion that is to be found much more commonly among devout nuns than among even the most dedicated of priests or monks.

There was also a peculiar preciousness I had never seen before. In private conversation it was expressed in a manner and diction that I can call only antique Mayfair on ice. His speech was not really like anything one ever heard either in Edinburgh or in London, yet it was both. It was certainly distinctive. In church it was startling. On Sunday evenings he sang Vespers (rare if not unique in Roman Catholic parishes in Scotland) in a tone that suggested a private duet with God that a few fortunate mortals were permitted to overhear. In his exquisitely intoned *Deus, in adjutorium meum intende?* not only could you hear the comma; you somehow knew you were expected to hear it and that anyone so unattuned to the heavenly music as not to hear it was being simultaneously cast into utter darkness.

He liked the Dominicans. Every Sunday, as far as possible, he had one preach either at High Mass or at Vespers. The homily was always, by Father Gray's choice, short. He listened intently to it as though savoring a wine, even though the vintage might not always be the best. His own sermons were as distinctive as was everything else about him. I suspect he did not much like preaching. In the pulpit he gave one the impression of his having descended from heaven with a condescension he had for long trained himself to disguise in the interests of missionary enterprise, using all the self-discipline at his command to hide his celestial origin, which nevertheless could not but show itself here and there, his valiant efforts notwithstanding. Peter Anson alludes to his "remarkably sensitive hands and an enigmatic smile reminiscent of . . . Mona Lisa"[3]—a peculiarly apt simile. The congregation of middle-class Edinburgh Catholics who listened, each in his or her chair or *prie-dieu* seemed aware that their priest was notably unlike other men, not even like other priests. And all the while, Marc-André Raffalovich would be in his *prie-dieu* near the altar rails, rapt in contemplation of the words of his pastor and greatest friend.

Gray's road to the priesthood is as complex as the man himself. The beginning of the decisive change in the orientation of his inner life came in 1889. It happened in Brittany, where he had been invited for a summer visit by a Catholic friend. His attraction to Rome could not be attributed to his witnessing any grandeur or beauty of liturgical ceremonial. On the contrary, what he saw was a wayside chapel, a few old women worshippers, and an ill-shaven priest notably hurried and careless in his celebration of the Mass. This, however, convinced John that he had seen "the real thing."[4]

His conversion at the time seemed to alter him little if at all, for he returned to his life as a decadent and dandy. But something must have germinated in him, for a few years later he was on his way to a radically new sort of life as a disciplined and dedicated priest, a path from which he never deviated.

John Gray, no doubt, must have seemed an unlikely candidate for the priesthood. Richard Le Gallienne appears to have been the one who introduced him to Oscar Wilde; still, this is not entirely clear. According to Rupert Croft-Cooke, Wilde picked Gray up in a bar in 1889. *The Daily Telegraph* reported a lecture of his delivered on February 7, 1892, under Wilde's chairmanship, calling Gray a protégé of Wilde, which Wilde disavowed in a letter to that paper on February 20.

There are indications that Wilde had intended to bear the cost of publishing Gray's first book of poems, *Silverpoints*, published in 1893 by Elkin Matthews and John Lane "at the sign of the Bodley Head," consisting of original poems and also translations from Charles Baudelaire, Stéphane Mallarmé, Paul Verlaine, and Arthur Rimbaud. If so, either he or Gray had a change of mind; at any rate, in the end John Lane (The Bodley Press) bore the whole cost[5]. The book, dedicated to Princess Alice of Monaco, was to have John Masefield among its admirers.

In 1892, another newspaper, *The Star*, identified Gray as the real-life original of Dorian in *The Picture of Dorian Gray*. Gray brought a libel suit against the Star for this allegation and won his case against the newspaper. Father Brocard Sewell, who has researched John Gray's early life extensively, reports, however, that in January 1961 a first edition of *The Picture of Dorian Gray* was offered for sale in New York containing a letter from John Gray to Oscar Wilde signed "Yours ever, Dorian." As Father Sewell remarks, "Had the existence of this letter been known to the *Star* people and to their lawyers the case might have been decided differently"[6] although the letter does not in itself prove that Dorian Gray was intended to be a portrait of John Gray. In the conviviality of the Rhymers' Club, it would have been natural for Gray to have been nicknamed Dorian. In the same year, the *annus mirabilis* of John's early literary period, he formed a friendship with Pierre Louÿs who took him to Paris, where he met Verlaine, Mallarmé, Marcel Schwob, and other Symbolist writers, and began writing for the Paris literary reviews of the day.

According to H. P. Clive, John Gray's relations with Pierre Louÿs "attained a high degree of intimacy." Clive quotes a letter from Louÿs

to Gray written in the summer of 1892 suggestive of this. Louÿs, on his
first visit to London, expressed delight at the refined manners of
Wilde's friends. Apparently he had not expected such elegance in
London. "These young people are most charming .... You can't
imagine the elegance of their manners." He cited, by way of example,
the action of one of them who, offering him a cigarette, first lighted it
and then offered it only after having taken the first puff himself. "Isn't
that exquisite?" he asked. Louÿs noted that they had even talked of a
marriage between two of them, with exchange of rings.

Such was the *ambiance* in which Gray found himself in the early
nineties. At this point Gray's conversion to Catholicism seems to have
had no detectable effect on his manner of life. For many of the
decadents of this period, among whom conversion to Rome was a sort
of fashion, the attraction to the Church was primarily if not entirely
aesthetic. Gray, however, as we shall see, seems to have experienced a
second and more serious conversion a few years later.

There can be no doubt at all that Gray lived in an atmosphere of *fin
de siècle* decadence in London and Paris, having been drawn into such
society in both cities through his literary associations. Father Sewell
calls *Silverpoints* "Beardsleyesque" and notes both the admiration Gray
received from the beautiful young Olive Custance, who later married
Lord Alfred Douglas in 1901, and Gray's susceptibility to feminine
beauty and charm. By the time I met Father Gray, evidence of any such
susceptibility had been for long rigorously hidden from his personality
and demeanor. I can only say that the solitary occasion on which I ever
saw him leave his customary pulpit rationality and calm for a histrionic
outburst was in a reference, which seemed to come out of the blue,
disconnected with the rest of his homily, in which he suddenly
inveighed with passionate excitement against those women who, he
said, "dance naked on a stage to drive men's souls to hell." It seemed at
the time out of character with most of his preaching and one could
sense a slight wave of astonishment passing through the rather douce
Edinburgh congregation at the unexpected allusion.

It was in these early years that Gray had formed the friendship with
Raffalovich that was to play such a permanent role in the lives of both.
They moved together in literary circles. They attended meetings of the
Theosophical Society in London together and went to séances (Gray
was also intersted in Swedenborg). Among the psychics they consulted
was Ailsa Cassilis, whom they met in 1895 and of whom Raffalovich
wrote that she "sat in Bond Street, semi-Sicilian, semi-Hindoo, and yet
blond, a rosy creature with spangles and sequins. For a sovereign she
held your hand for a quarter of an hour or so, and prattled prettily
about you."[8] Both men were keen students of parapsychological

phenomena at that time. The large number of psychics they knew included Cheiro, a fashionable practitioner of palmistry at that time, who prophesied that Oscar Wilde would die in prison: a prediction that was not strictly fulfilled, since Wilde died in Paris in 1900, three years after his release from Reading Gaol, but was nevertheless remarkable.

In 1895, Raffalovich published a little book in French, *L'Affaire Oscar Wilde*, which was reprinted the following year as part of a book he published on homosexuality, *Uranisme et unisexualité,* a pioneer work in its day, quoted by Havelock Ellis in his *The Psychology of Sex*, 1897. Raffalovich's book is now so rare that even the British Museum has no copy of it. There is one, however, in the National Library of Scotland. The author, after his conversion to Catholicism, spent much time and money recalling copies and destroying them.

Raffalovich was beyond question homosexually oriented as, of course, were Wilde and many other members of the circle in which Gray moved. Whether Gray himself was so oriented cannot be definitely established one way or another, such strong circumstantial evidence notwithstanding. At one point Raffalovich warned Gray against association with Wilde and eventually issued a sort of ultimatum to the effect that Gray must choose between him and Wilde. Gray eventually chose Raffalovich's friendship.

The arrest of Wilde in 1895 may have had a devastating effect on Gray. There is a story, based only on the testimony of one of the converts he made in later life, that, one morning in London, Gray received some news that shocked him and that he went into a little church in Leicester Place dedicated to Notre Dame de France to pray before an image of the Virgin Mother. He thought he had been at prayer for only a normal length of time when the church began to grow dark and an old woman appeared, ready to close it. He had been there all day.

Gray was a very complex character. His sister, Sister Mary Raphael, relates that when he was a young man, John was much interested in black people, which was unexpected in a man of Gray's time, temper, and milieu. Gray went so far as to say that, although he was a white man, he felt black inside and predicted that one day the black race would rule the world. He also had a special liking for St. Sebastian, who in legend was shot by arrows and is so depicted in Christian art. Both Wilde and Raffalovich apparently shared this interest as well.

In 1898, on October 25, John Gray took up residence at the Scots College, Rome, as a candidate for the priesthood, the very place where the ill-starred and unhappy genius Frederick Rolfe (known better to a literary posterity as "Baron Corvo") had tried his vocation a decade earlier. Gray was ordained to the priesthood on December 21, 1901, by

Cardinal Respighi in the Lateran Basilica. The following year he was a curate in the slum parish of St. Patrick's, Edinburgh, where, according to all who knew him then, he was outstandingly diligent in humble pastoral service to the parishioners. A few years later, however, with Raffalovich nearby, he conceived and built the remarkable church to which I alluded at the outset. In the adjoining clergy house, built to seem modest but tastefully appointed, he lived somewhat like a Renaissance prelate trying to give the impression of inconspicuousness. There, at St. Peter's, Father Gray continued his pastoral work with no less dedication than before but now with the moral, cultural, and financial support of his wealthy and intelligent patron and admirer.

Raffalovich endeavored to hold court in his handsome and secluded house (one of the largest of a number of dignified stone villas in a pleasant district known as "The Grange" on the south side of Edinburgh), as far as possible in the manner in which he had conducted his *salons* in Paris when he and Father Gray had been young men. Rarely did anyone of literary or artistic importance who visited Edinburgh fail to be invited to Raffy's home, where his guests included Henry James, Max Beerbohm, Hilaire Belloc, Arthur Symons, Eric Gill (who like Gray was a member of the Third Order of St. Dominic), Gordon Bottomley, and Compton Mackenzie, author of *Whisky Galore* or, as it was known in America, *Tight Little Island*. Needless to say, Gray found solace in the enjoyment of convivial converse with such distinguished figures in the world of art and letters.

The two old friends saw one another almost daily during the more than a quarter-century of Father Gray's incumbency. Gray usually went on foot (he was an enthusiastic walker), Raffalovich by horsecab or, in later years, taxi. The utmost decorum was always maintained between them. That there was a homosexual relationship between them has often been alleged or suggested in literary circles in London and elsewhere. Such gossip was no doubt inevitable. Henry James alluded to it, perhaps not entirely without relish.

Father Sewell thinks it "for more than one reason improbable." As already mentioned it could never even have occurred to me when I knew Father Gray; but even in retrospect I am inclined to think Father Sewell's skepticism well founded. Plainly, there is no way of proving or disproving the allegations fostered by such gossip. I can only say with him that they seem, for various reasons, unlikely to have any basis in fact.

There is no doubt, however, that before Gray met Raffalovich in 1892, he was living beyond his means and was at one time even in danger of arrest for debt. He would have been a monster of ingratitude had he not remained a loyal friend of the benefactor who had not only rescued him from poverty but established him in a life that so graciously fulfilled his priestly ideals.

Father Gray entertained a remarkable variety of people at the rectory, many of them unusually interesting. He served china tea—one cup only. In his social life as in his liturgical duties, everything was done with clockwork precision. Edinburgh manners in those day were notably formal. Neighbors who had known each other and lived beside each other for thirty or forty years addressed each other by title and surname till the day of death; indeed after death, too, for I have heard pious utterances such as "The undertakers will be coming for Lady Smith in a few minutes" and even prayers such as "We thank Thee that Colonel Brown is now in Thy nearer presence." Unlike the French, who honor their dead by instantly omitting all earthly titles (on the plausible view that matters may be differently arranged on the other side of the veil), the Edinburgh citizens of the day, in speaking of the dead, invested their most recent titles with a tone of macabre finality, as though in the life everlasting they would remain for ever "Captain" or "Miss" or "Major" or "Marquis" or "Chief Petty Officer." Not even the Swedes, known for their preoccupation with titles, could have taken such designations with such seriousness as to send souls forth on death labeled with the particular title they had happened to hold at their last breath. Even a highly intelligent priest such as Gray was not unaffected by such usage.

To that customary northern formality, however, Gray brought two further formidable dimensions: (1) the Byzantine grandeur of the Roman liturgy in those days long before Vatican II had depreciated it and (2) the half-mocking, aloof politeness that made the *fin de siècle* live on in him a generation after it had vanished in almost everybody else. Rarely have I known anyone so completely a period piece. Besides, his exquisiteness was reinforced by his having sanctified it as part of the manner of life he had chosen in becoming a priest. Sometimes he seemed a dandy with a halo.

Moray McLaren, a gifted Scottish writer, relates two stories that illustrate John Gray's style of conversation and behavior. Raffy had asked Moray McLaren, then a young man, to be so good as to take Father Gray for a walk over the Border hills. Gray, an accomplished hiker, walked with him in silence for an hour. They both enjoyed the beautiful day. At last the younger man tried desperately to break the now embarrassing silence by means of a trite observation on the fine view. To this Father Gray responded with a bleak smile, "Chatterbox!"

Another hour or so passed. At last Gray gently intoned, "Come, come, young Mr. McLaren, I am told that you are a witty and paradoxical conversationalist. I am waiting to be amused."

The other, even funnier and more characteristic, story relates to an invitation Gray had extended to a priest from Cornwall to give a series of sermons at St. Peter's. Seated at the dining room table, which was splendidly set out with the finest of napery, crystal, and silver, Gray said to his guest, "Father, you must be tired after your long journey. May I offer you the refreshment of the wine of the country?"

So saying, he poured out into a wine glass some of the rarest malt whisky obtainable in the world, handed it to his guest and proceeded to talk with his customary vivacity and elegance. Alas, his guest's fatigue had not been underestimated. In reaching out for the glass, the visitor spilled its contents all over the impeccably appointed table. At this, Gray merely pulled the bell. A maid entered. Gray made an inconspicuous gesture in silence and she no less silently retreated, then brought an assistant maid to help her reset the table exactly as it had been. This process naturally took some time, during which Gray simply went on talking grandly.

Then, as the servants had finished and left the room, Gray, as if reminding himself of something he had foolishly forgotten, broke off his discourse and exclaimed, "Forgive me Father, you must be tired after your long journey. May I offer you the refreshment of the wine of the country?"[9]

In such old-fashioned formality, André readily cooperated. Each day, when Gray called on him, a servant would announce, "Father Gray is here," and André would jump up with a look of mild surprise as if his parish priest were making an annual visitation rather than a daily visit.

In 1930, Father Gray became a canon of the Cathedral. Thereafter he was always alluded to in the third person as "The Canon" and addressed, of course, as "Canon Gray"; the title became inextricably woven into him. One day, in conversation, I inadvertently addressed him as "Monsignor." I don't know why I made the slip; I certainly knew better. I recognized it as soon as it fell from my lips. I was completely unprepared, however, for the extraordinary effect it produced. He shot me a quick, hurt (perhaps almost frightened) glance. Then he drew himself up with all the majestic *hauteur* at his command and, with a countenance that had grown gradually purple as we spoke, he moved slowly away with elegant dignity. The reaction seemed to me excessive for what was plainly a very young man's slip of the tongue. What lay behind this overreaction I can only surmise. Perhaps he detected some hint of mockery welling up from my unconscious and so imputed to me an attempt to ridicule him. There may have been more, however, to his strange reaction, a background beyond my ken. It does suggest, of course, an overconcern for ecclesiastical rank such as one would not expect in a priest who was a man of letters. One must not forget, however, that for both him and his friend, Edinburgh was a retreat from the world, a total break from the past. Formality assisted them.

Gray was certainly a man of letters. Although he published nothing from the time he became rector of St. Peter's till 1921, the corpus of his published writings is of high quality on the whole. Except for a few devotional writings, a strange novel called *Park*, some essays and short stories, and a brief description of his church published by Basil Blackwell in 1925 in an edition limited to 500 copies, much of his work consists of poetry. Two of his poems are to be found in *The Oxford Book of English Mystical Verse*: "The Tree of Knowledge" and "On the Holy Trinity." The latter speaks of a desert, whose "way is wonderfully strange," into which God leads the soul. The poems contain echoes from both John of the Cross and Francis Thompson.

Gray's *genre* of poetry was always in some sense mystical, whether he were writing in a specifically Catholic mood or otherwise. He was a mystic by temperament. He enjoyed the beauties of nature, especially in her manifestations of peace and solitude, in soft meadow or on snow-clad mountain, while resolutely binding himself to the narrower and, to him, still deeper grasp of God, through service to Him in the ancient liturgy of the Church and the chores of urban and suburban parish life.

When Gray was a young man in London, a group of up-and-coming poets, rebels against the literary establishment of the day, met regularly in a pub called "The Cheshire Cheese," calling themselves "The Rhymers' Club." Gray, though apparently not a member, was regularly invited and his poems of that period reflect the symbolist influence of the contemporaries whose work he admired. They have a distinctive tone that makes them strange today even to those familiar with the hothouse accents of poets of that milieu.

Lionel Johnson wrote Gray off as "a sometimes beautiful oddity; not more." From today's perspective, however, I think we may write off that remark in turn as the pique of a rival. Members of such coteries tend to spend much of their time trying to find something witty to say about the others and the wit tends to be feline. One may happen to have no liking for Gray's precious style. It has, however, literary merit and an originality that many better-known poets might well covet. Gray, from his postconversion standpoint, regretted his entire output pertaining to that period. He bought up copies of *Silverpoints*, poems he had inscribed to contemporaries such as Oscar Wilde, Paul Verlaine, Frank Harris, Ernest Dowson, and Ellen Terry, the actress.

Verlaine, in an exquisitely anguished poem, *Sagesse*, had asked

himself what he had done with his youth.[10] Gray was, among poets of
that circle, perhaps the one who had least reason to weep in answering
that question. For whatever his youth had been, he certainly redeemed
it in his more than thirty years of life as an exemplary parish priest. Yet
he did not by any means forget the friends of those early days. He
helped to guide Beardsley toward the Catholic faith and, once a year at
St. Peter's, Edinburgh, the name of Paul Verlaine was commemorated
in prayer. That kind of faithfulness does breathe an *odor sanctitatis*.

Father Gray was a master of charitable rebuke. I recall an occasion
on which he was showing me, as a boy of eighteen, some vestments in
the sacristy. As we entered he noticed an amice and some other things
lying in disarray as if thrown down in a hurry. Uttering one of his
inimitably restrained sighs, he murmured softly, "What dogs they are!"
It was an allusion, of course, to the popular name of the Order of
Preachers: *Domini canes*, the Lord's dogs. But in his voice was no
vestige of contempt or hostility. His tone was more that of an old-
fashioned schoolma'am on discovering an act of boyish thoughtlessness
in one of her favorite pupils. And always the mysterious Mona-Lisa
smile. It was almost as though he were trying out new ways of
moderating the aloofness he felt he must observe.

Everything he did was done too perfectly. He talked almost as a
foreign expert linguist speaks English, using a construction and an
accent so impeccable that no native speaker would ever so sound. His
speech and his mannerisms were so crisp, so precious, that once you
had heard the former and seen the latter, everybody else's seemed just a
little sloppy at best. Yet it was all done with such skill that it never
seemed artificial so long as you were in his company. Only when you
had not been with him for some time might it seem in retrospect odd. It
was not an affected sort of speech. It seemed quite natural, but natural
only to him. If someone were to call me and mimic Gray's tone of
voice—were there still people with sufficient knowledge of him and of
such dramatic talent—I think I might almost jump out of my skin with
shock. I believe, however, that I am pretty safe from hearing that
singularly inimitable speech again.

I once heard him at an evening service, discoursing on the fact that
the Mass is the Mass no matter where it is said and by what priest. "A
priest may be John Smith who has certain characteristics and perhaps
plays a good game of tennis, but at the altar he is sunk in anonymity as
the celebrant." He went on to invite us, his hearers, to look around the
church and appreciate its beauty. Nevertheless, he insisted, no beauty,
no grandeur, no pomp, no majesty, could be adequate for the
celebration of so awesome a mystery. He spoke of the early Church in

Rome, of the practice of having seven deacons assisting in the Holy Sacrifice and he asserted that even that was far too meager an honor to fit the worship of the King of Kings, the offering to God of his own Son in the Mass. Some dimensions of the Christian faith seemed to have eluded Father Gray entirely, but what he grasped he grasped in a uniquely elegant manner and he gave to it a punctilious devotion rare in even the most devout of priests.

In private conversation, he always treated me with icy reserve, yet all the while he seemed to be trying to help me, if from the infinite distance of his heart. He spoke always as a churchman, as a priest. Nothing ever seemed to surprise him; he was too far away, too detached from everything that was not pinned securely to the Church. So, at any rate, it seemed, and such is the testimony of those who knew him much better than I. Perhaps if I had had the faintest inkling of his past life and could have understood it adequately at the time, I might have detected in him a constant vigilance over ghosts that still haunted him out of a bygone London and Paris.

A young Belgian to whom I casually showed a picture of Gray in an Edinburgh newspaper remarked simply, "Eh voilà un chic type!" That was what so often showed through his icily clerical demeanor. Yet in retrospect one cannot but wonder whether the *chic type* in him were not itself a veil over a still earlier John Gray, who had toiled in his teens as a metal worker in London to help eke out the family budget.

Which was the real John Gray? Perhaps by the time I knew him even he did not quite know which was his "real" self. Rather, he knew only that his transformed self was the best and that he must persist in it with superhuman fidelity and perseverance. It represented the values I admired in him more than his elegance or wit. I can see now that I was right, for the latter were mere propensities; the former were achievements. Had I known about him then what I have since learned, perhaps he would not have seemed quite so uncannily inscrutable. I fancy, however, that on the whole this would have been a pity. It is better to know it only now, when his spirit has fled the earth on which he walked so strangely.

André Raffalovich died on Ash Wednesday, February 14, 1934. The previous evening he had attended a lecture at the College of Art by his friend Eric Gill, who was staying at the rectory. He was discovered in his room when the taxi came for him, as it did every morning to take him to Mass at St. Peter's. He was seventy-three. "The Canon" was sent for and arrived at once to give conditional absolution and extreme unction. He then returned to St. Peter's to bless the ashes with which, on that first day of Lent, the foreheads of the faithful are signed with the smudge of the Cross.[11] Then he said Mass as usual.

The day of the funeral was bitterly cold and "The Canon" characteristically wore nothing over the customary vestments. He took ill afterwards and never recovered. Having contracted pleurisy and developed an abscess in his lung, he was operated on. The operation was too much for him. On June 14, four months after the death of his friend, John Gray died, his last words an act of contrition.

At the requiem in a crowded St. Peter's, his Dominican friend, Father Bernard Delany, said, "He made songs and sang as a poet; but it is the songs and the poems he did *not* sing that gave him his real, his royal, priestly greatness . . . . How many songs must die that the supreme song of self-dedication must live?" That goes indeed to the heart of the mystery of John Gray; perhaps to the mystery of all of us.

So was laid to rest this singular man and still more singular priest. I can hardly now regret that I knew him less well than I might have wished for, through his aloof reticence and chill dignity, I learned something of the cost of a mystic's dedication to his priestly office, and from that lesson, I learned also to pity the loneliness of his pilgrimage and to admire the greatness of the pilgrim who made it.

I add only one very personal story: to me a deeply significant one. In 1928, when I was barely eighteen, not very long after I had begun to make the acquaintance of Father Gray, I happened to be in London and was studying a map to find directions to some place to which I wished to go. Suddenly my eye caught the indication of a church in Leicester Place. I looked it up in a guide book and saw it was called Notre Dame de France.[12] Unaccountably, I was seized by an overpowering and inexplicable desire to visit the church and did so. Of course, when I went to this church under this strange impulse, I had not the slightest notion of any connection or association with Father Gray, who was far from my mind at the time. I was entirely ignorant, not only of his day-long vigil there more than thirty years earlier, but of all else in Gray's early life. Neither before my visit nor for many decades thereafter could I discern any plausible reason why I should have had that uncanny, compelling urge. If I were to look for one now, almost sixty years later, it would have to be in the domain of parapsychological phenomena.

When I knew John Gray in the late twenties and early thirties, not only was his early life in London and Paris in the days of Wilde and Louÿs completely unknown to me, I believe very few people, who knew him only as a reserved and disciplined priest as I did, had any inkling of his history. I recall some vague rumors that he had been a wealthy English convert who had built St. Peter's with his own money: a garbled story if ever there were one, not to say a travesty of the facts.

Few outside his own most intimate circle seemed to know anything

much of his considerable literary output. I chanced upon some of it
merely by accident. Today he has become a literary cult, bidding fair
to rival the cult of Corvo, a very different personality indeed, yet with
some things in common with Gray. Scholars are now writing articles
about Gray's work and graduate students are researching it. Yet if he
had written nothing at all and remained entirely obscure, the memory
of this elegantly anachronistic priest, this lonely, lonely man prancing
down the nave of his unique church administering the Asperges before
High Mass with a dour Presbyterian Edinburgh encompassing yet
sheltering him like a dark cloud, would have haunted me to the end of
my days.

> phrases of familiar words
> It is just a rock scratching.
> You will sympathise with
> the emotion the author
> experienced in hearing the
> poems spoken by children
> in the Cowgate dialect
> Yours very sincerely
>   John Gray

John Gray

Charles Warr greeting H.M. the Queen

TWO

Charles Laing Warr

Charles Laing Warr (1892-1969) was closely associated with the British royal family from his boyhood. His father, Alfred, a Londoner by birth, became the incumbent of Rosneath, a West Highland parish in Scotland. It was located on a peninsula that belonged almost entirely to the eighth duke of Argyll, whose son, the Marquis of Lorne, had married Queen Victoria's fourth daughter, the Princess Louise. The princess had a great affection for Charles as a little boy, whom she called her adopted child, and her influence affected his whole life.

Warr, after completing his university degree, sought and obtained a commission as an officer in the 9th Argyll and Sutherland Highlanders in World War I. Severely wounded in the second battle of Ypres in 1915, he was eventually invalided after comparatively brief active service. In those days, a wartime officer's life expectancy was a few months, yet Charles survived. During his convalescence, feeling he had been miraculously spared, he resolved that he had been called to better things than the slaughter of his fellow men. He renounced his ambitions for a career at the Scottish Bar and, following in his father's footsteps, entered the ministry of the Scottish Kirk at the University of Glasgow Divinity Hall.

After spending several years in a parish of his own, Warr was suddenly catapulted into the pulpit of Scotland's premier kirk, St. Giles' Cathedral, Edinburgh. Shortly afterwards, in 1926, largely because of the Princess Louise's influence, King George V appointed him to the two separate offices of Dean of the Order of Thistle (the Scottish counterpart to the Order of the Garter) and Dean of the Chapel Royal in Scotland.

The appointment of a man in his early thirties to such a notably central position in the Church of Scotland and British society was, in those days, viewed with widespread astonishment and alarm. Charles never entirely lived down the resentment it caused among his more mature contemporaries, but he persevered and served with great distinction. St. Giles' had been for long at the heart of Scottish life and for longer still the focus of much of Scotland's stormy history. Charles became a favorite and confidant of several generations of the royal family, from George V, who called him his Boy Dean, to the present Queen who, at a private investiture at Windsor Castle shortly before Warr's death, made him the first Scottish clergyman to receive the Grand Cross of the Royal Victorian Order, bestowed for personal services to the Sovereign.

Charles, despite his being accounted by superficial observers something of an Edwardian period piece, was intensely human and loving, a true friend to those he cherished and a stalwart foe of all that he deemed mean or base. No scholar in any academic sense, he was nevertheless notably cultured and gifted, with a discriminating taste in literature, music and the visual arts.

No one who imagines that personal dignity cannot be accompanied by love and laughter could ever have known Charles Warr. When he died, people of all classes lined the streets of Edinburgh to pay their last respects to a great man as his funeral cortège passed by. Warr's life and work have been commemorated by the Very Reverend Dr. Ronald Selby Wright in the *Dictionary of National Biography*.

You always pray for Lilibet; you never pray for me.
—Princess Margaret (as a child) to Dr. Warr.

Never in all my life have I known a man at once so lovable and yet so misunderstood as Charles Warr. His endearing warmheartedness and intense loyalty to his friends, even his keen and sometimes uproarious sense of humor, were to many observers hidden under an old-fashioned, formalistic dignity of manner. The mask he adopted in public was due partly to his awareness of his short physical stature and partly to his love of ceremony. But it can be better understood when one knows his early background.

One of the great influences upon Charles was his boyhood "adoption" by Princess Louise. He always depicted the Princess as having been as informal as any princess in those days could possibly have dared to be: a strong, handsome, approachable woman with a delightfully robust, even mischievous sense of humor. No doubt his ideals in later life had been molded by his memories of this lady, whose

ways belonged to a courtly age that had all but passed by the time
Charles was beginning his career. Nevertheless, when her outlook was
translated into his attitudes in the transitional period between the two
world wars, it gave to many (alas, how wrongly!) the impression of a
stuffiness that was alien to Charlie's loving heart and openness of
mind.

King George's decision to appoint Charles Warr, then the incumbent
at St. Giles' Cathedral, to the office of Dean of the Order of the Thistle
and of the Chapel Royal, in 1926, was largely influenced by Princess
Louise. She had been pouring the praises of her protégé into the King's
ear for a decade and, when the appointments fell vacant, the King
insisted on giving them to Charles. In those days, Britain's was still the
empire on which the sun never set. For such a young man to be
suddenly catapulted into these two royal offices seemed to many a
dazzling leap to fame. Naturally, many who thought they had been
passed over were disgruntled. Some dignitaries even made their
annoyance public. One of them went so far as to write to the King to
inquire whether he had not made a mistake!

When one considers the character of the age and the nature of the
circumstances, one can well understand that it would have been
remarkable if such a young man's head had not been turned by such a
meteoric rise to prominence. Though only thirty-three at the time, his
head was in fact turned remarkably little. In later years, he always
accounted himself unusually favored by good fortune. He had no
illusions about his own limitations, but he had an immense, perhaps an
exaggerated, sense of the importance of his offices, which many
interpreted, quite wrongly, as a sense of his own importance.

True, Warr was a perfervid royalist, perhaps *plus royaliste que le
roi*, in a day when his particular kind of royalism had become, even
among the most ardent supporters of the British monarchy, a little
old-fashioned. He was temperamentally a mixture of Edwardian and
late Victorian. To many, even in conservative Edinburgh, he came to
be regarded as something of a period piece. If he was perhaps indeed
such a period piece, he was a very fine one, a link with the best of the
age that had passed away. He was not a scholar in any strict sense, but
he was both intelligent and delightfully cultivated.

His drawing-room walls were covered with signed photographs and
other mementoes from kings and queens. This display was due partly
to his natural inclination to honor the donors of such tributes of royal
affection by so honoring them in return, but far, far more to a genuine
affection for the members of the royal family he had come to know.
Charles loved all sorts and conditions of men and if people in high
places chose to express their love of him he instinctively returned their

love. At Christmastide, he would lift a card from a side table and say
in his elegant way, "From Queen Mary. She always sends her flower
garden. A lovely idea, don't you think?"

The royal family trusted him, no doubt because he was open, frank
and decisive. He did not engage in intricate intrigue or go obliquely
about his aims. They could rely on him because they understood and
liked him. But Charles was also a good pastor in his old-fashioned
way. Perhaps his best friends were mostly from the highest and the
lowest orders of society. Too many of those in between suspected him
because they did not understand the simple frankness of his nature. Yet
no one could have had a better or more loyal friend than Charles
Warr.

I first made the acquaintance of Dr. Warr in 1939 when I was in my
final year as a theological student in Edinburgh. As a result of
recommendations he had received from various sources, he decided to
consider me for an appointment as assistant minister at St. Giles'
Cathedral, which was to fall vacant in June of that year. I had never
applied for the position, nor had I ever met Warr before he invited me
to read one of the lessons on Sunday morning and to have lunch with
him afterwards at the Manse, a dignified townhouse in
Northumberland Street on Edinburgh's north side.

Before lunch, he handed me several Sunday newspapers, including
The Observer, and asked me to bear with his absence for a few
minutes. On his return some considerable time later, he apologized
courteously and we went into lunch where, after grace, he began
immediately to ask my views on world events. From that time
throughout the two years I was with him at St. Giles', he always
seemed to expect of me a greater knowledge of current events than I
believed my experience warranted. Apparently the fact that I had lived
in and traveled much of continental Europe disposed him to think I
ought to have a feel for its pulse. By this time Munich was a recent and
macabre memory, for Hitler had just marched into Czechoslovakia and
at last everybody saw, however reluctantly, that we were on the verge
of war. I had spent six months at Heidelberg University the previous
year and had returned just before Munich. Warr knew this and also
that I had lived much in France and Belgium. He talked to me as
though I ought to be an expert in foreign affairs. It was his way of
informally examining me for the position for which he was considering
me.

After lunch, he continued the conversation more and more affably
in the drawing room, where at length he simply asked me if June would
be a convenient month for me to begin duties. I said it would be and
thus began two years of a remarkably exciting appointment for a
young man.

Three months later Neville Chamberlain made his radio announcement on the morning of September 3, 1939: Britain was at war with Germany. I had been in London the previous week and managed to get back to Edinburgh by train. Warr had been on holiday and he too had returned to Edinburgh in time for the Sunday morning service at St. Giles'. The hymns had been selected before the declaration of war. One of them was the hymn whose first line reads, "Glorious things of thee are spoken," admirably suitable except that it is traditionally sung to Haydn's tune widely associated with *Deutschland, Deutschland uberalles.* Although an imperfectly suppressed wry smile was to be seen on some faces, Warr's was conspicuously controlled. The sadness in all hearts dominated everything else.

As a result of his battle service in World War I, which had almost cost him an arm, Warr was prey throughout the rest of his life to a septic condition with high fever. By the end of 1939, when I had become senior assistant at the cathedral, his sudden indispositions caused him to call upon me to deputize for him on many occasions, usually on short notice. I did so, for example, at the memorial service for John Buchan, Lord Tweedsmuir, Governor-General of Canada, the Scottish counterpart of the service held simultaneously at Westminster Abbey.

On Easter Eve that year Warr called me on the telephone to say that he could not be at church on Easter morning and I must take over both the celebration of Holy Communion and the Easter sermon, a formidable responsibility for a young man ordained only a few months earlier to the ministry of the Scottish Kirk. Not only was I unprepared, but I had to face a vast congregation including many dignitaries and some of my own recent theological professors. In such exigencies Warr never failed to cheer me with encouragement beforehand and tales of widespread approval afterwards about the way I had preached and functioned. He was always a thoroughly kind and compassionate man while at the same time never letting me forget that he was my commanding officer.

At the staff meeting every Tuesday morning, he received my report for the week, which included an account of my pastoral visits. I was responsible for visiting at least twenty-five families each week, which sometimes included a remarkable variety of people, for the congregation spanned every social class in the city from the abject poor in the immediate neighborhood of the ancient church to Lords of the Court of Session. My duties took me both to the homes of Edinburgh's affluent and privileged families and to the dark and dismal tenements of the Canongate and High Street, including hundreds of interesting families and individuals who belonged to neither social extreme.

Warr never entirely accustomed himself to the changes that had taken place in Britain since his Edwardian youth. He expected in all things a grandeur and a gaiety of spirit such as had been so much a part of British social life before the carnage of World War I. His hospitality was always generous and I was very frequently a recipient of it at the Manse. His wife, "Ruby," (Christian Lawson Aitken, whom he had married in 1918), suffered from a hyperthyroid condition with exophthalmia that gave her eyes a bulging, fearsome look. They had no children. He always seemed to treat her with respect and kindness. He sometimes called her "Dinky", a name that was hardly apposite, since her figure by then was anything other than trim, but she was a lovable person and the pet name expressed, no doubt, Warr's typical loyalty to the past. They seemed to love each other very much.

To compensate for his selfconsciousness about the shortness of his stature, he adopted a somewhat Napoleonic mien, intimidating to many, infuriating to some. Yet how thin was the mask! As soon as he took to you it seemed to melt like a glister of ice on a spring morning. His smile was almost babylike, his chuckle completely disarming and infectiously warm. When I first knew him he was still only in his late forties and full of energy and bounce, yet his impressive brow was bald and his hair white and curly at the back, giving rise to apocryphal stories about kind old ladies offering to help him across the street. Very rarely was he to be seen without his clerical collar, beneath which glowed a purple stock neatly tucked into his black waistcoat. He was always dressed in well-tailored clothes of the best possible quality and his hands elegantly manicured.

All that sounds dull enough and might have been so in fact but for the extraordinary light that streamed from his blue eyes; his gaze, whenever he was animated and pleased, seemed to pour forth all the love and tenderness he was afraid to show the world at large. The mask he habitually wore for public view was assumed, contrary to widespread belief, because of an intense sensitivity. He longed for genuine love and friendship and was so afraid of hostility that he too often and too much disguised the warmth and radiance of his own personality. I do not think I have met anyone else whose eyes glowed so warmly with love and laughter; but before you could possibly be in the way of seeing it happen, he had to be absolutely certain that you would not trespass on his soul, which he guarded as private sanctuary. Even when he knew you well and loved you, the slightest suggestion of trespass brought up the drawbridge and left you with a wide moat. Then suddenly you perceived that the sunshine had gone, hid behind a dark, impenetrable cloud, which was always so sad, because the sunshine of his presence was deep refreshment to the soul.

Although Charles did not think of himself as having powers of the
highest literary level, he loved to write and began doing so early. His
first book, *The Unseen Host*, written after he had been invalided out of
the army at the age of twenty-three, went into ten editions. It was
followed by several novels and nonfiction books, including an
historical defense of the Scottish Kirk. In 1960, the year before his
wife's death, he published his last book, *The Glimmering Landscape*. A
memoir of his own life, it contains much information about the many
interesting and illustrious people he had known in the course of his
long ministry. The churl who found (or pretended to find) it a parade
of name-dropping could not have more grievously misunderstood
Charles Warr.

Whatever his faults, snobbery was not one of them. Ever since his
boyhood, Charles had learned to admire royalty and sympathize with
its problems. He was for many years a close friend of George V, whom
he especially admired. They probably shared the same instincts and
outlook. Warr, like that king, had great dignity on the outside yet a
deep simplicity when relaxing among close friends at his own fireside.
That was what made him punctilious on ceremonial occasions yet able
to feel at home with humble folk and cheer them with his simple fun.
Although he did love coronets, it was for the kind hearts he saw in
their wearers. I remember once mentioning to him a man of very
aristocratic lineage whose manners seemed to belie it. Charles looked
up with a merry smile, whispering, "Yes, isn't he dreadful?" Perhaps he
was too optimistic in his expectations of people, especially of the
well-born. If so, it but added to his charm.

A man's character may be seen in the people he most admires. Warr
admired courage and simplicity of heart. His battle wounds helped him
to recognize and admire the heart of a true soldier. He immensely
admired, for instance, a book by Donald Hankey, *A Student in Arms*.
Hankey was killed in action on October 26, 1916, and his book
expressed in a moving, although now very old-fashioned way, the
simple nobility of heart, the lofty ideals, and the cool courage with
which the flower of a nation's manhood faced the unspeakable carnage
and horror of war. That was what Charles understood and all soldiers
from generals to corporals instantly detected his understanding.

Charles admired talent of any kind, not least in the arts, especially
painting, sculpture, music and drama. He had a flair for drama.
Sometimes when it was my turn to preach at St. Giles' he would say
with a smile in his eyes, "I hope you're feeling nervous!" He felt that no
performer could ever do his best unless he felt some nervousness before
the performance.

He loved to talk to and to entertain actors and actresses at the manse. I once arrived there just as Dame Sybil Thorndike was about to take her leave with one of her two sons. Charles greeted me with an ebullient "Have you seen *The Corn Is Green*? If not, you are in disgrace." Fortunately I had and was thereupon presented to a delighted and amused Dame Sybil. Charles had a knack of saying the right thing at the right time. His flatteries were always courteous, never fulsome and rarely direct.

When the future Queen Elizabeth and her sister Princess Margaret were children, Princess Margaret, after a service at St. Giles', complained in her then girlish voice, "You *always* pray for Lilibet. You *never* pray for me."

Warr batted not an eyelid. As gravely as though he were addressing the General Assembly, he looked straight into the little girl's eyes and said, "Your Royal Highness is right. And in future, when we pray for your sister, Her Royal Highness the Princess Elizabeth, we shall always also pray for *you*, the Princess Margaret Rose." And so we always did.

Warr's churchmanship, though many accounted it Erastian, was much like that of the Anglican broad churchmen of an earlier day, but his private tastes inclined him to Catholic ceremonial, so far as Scottish Presbyterian tradition could accommodate it. He trained all the Cathedral staff to do everything "decently and in order." More than once he remarked unfavorably on those clergy who were slovenly in their dress in church. "They would not so attend a royal levée, if they were invited, " remarked Warr, "yet they so enter the house of the King of Kings."

Service at St. Giles' in Warr's day was conducted with Swiss-clock precision. We emerged from a side chapel, said prayer with the assembled choir; the procession had to have reached a certain point exactly on the hour. The old beadle (verger) who led us in procession was apparently, however, beyond Warr's teaching powers. He walked ahead of us in a sort of sailor's roll, the silver-topped wand swaying from left to right as though the cathedral nave were indeed a ship afloat on a stormy sea. Only now and then, in moments of exasperation Warr would say privately, "It's like walking behind the pendulum of a grandfather clock." The beadle in question was faithful but not very bright. He could never quite get the distinction between a cassock and a hassock and would occasionally ask a visiting clergyman if he had remembered to bring his hassock: an inquiry that evoked a mixture of anxiety and astonishment. He was eventually succeeded, after my time, by a wand bearer of military carriage and ceremonial precision.

Of course a man of Warr's temper and upbringing is likely to have many prejudices. He certainly had a large collection of them; but they were mostly very endearing ones and all understandable in the light of his upbringing and love of a bygone age. Yet when he could be made to see the practical advantage of a new outlook or new way of doing things, he would accept it cheerfully enough, if a little wistfully, so long as he could contrive to fit it into his general scheme of things. Somehow, once one became accustomed to his world, one could enter into the spirit of his prejudices and even make them one's own, at least pro tem.

He was not really annoyed at what went against his prejudices, only bewildered and slightly amused. He was much more easily annoyed by stupidity and especially by lack of common sense. He once told me of an assistant he had had in the past (he never identified the subject of such adverse criticism) who had asked him, "What does one say to a person when one makes a sick call?" "I told him," said Warr, "You say what you feel. What do you say to your auntie when she is sick?"

Even more rarely did he show outright anger, but I do recall one occasion on which Ruby came into his office almost in tears because some officious young woman in the military bureaucracy had been saucy to her. Warr's face flushed momentarily a gallant purple. He picked up the telephone and after he had tracked down the culprit, he wiped an imaginary floor with her so decisively and in such short order that I suspect she would be for some time anticipating summary court-martial and would be eventually astonished and grateful that it had not occurred.

When he retired from his incumbency of St. Giles', he was succeeded by a man of an entirely different stamp. They could not in the least understand each other and much bitterness developed between them, a bitterness that was well known in Edinburgh society which is much accustomed to such feuds. ("Put two Scots in an empty room and they fight over the furniture.") Probably few really knew how much this distressed Charles, who always set out with the expectation of being friends with all with whom he would be in any way associated. Only when he felt insulted did his resentment grow into bitterness. He kept, of course, his royal appointments, which were for life, and faithfully discharged the duties attached to them. The Queen gave him a "Grace and Favour" residence at her disposal in Moray Place, Edinburgh, an elegant and commodious townhouse where he remained for the rest of his life. Whenever my wife and I visited him there, after we had come to reside in the United States, he entertained us with his customarily lavish hospitality and always seemed immensely pleased that we came to see him. Once or twice I asked if he might not sometime visit America, but he pooh-poohed the suggestion as impracticable. He said he felt too old and could not endure the heat that he understood was one of the torments of life in the United States. So he never did tread American soil.

On March 8, 1967, just before his seventy-fifth birthday and two years before his death, he wrote me:

> I don't know whether I told you, but The Queen has made me a most gracious gesture. Instead of having to attend one of the Investitures, she has said that she would like to give me the Insignia of a G.C.V.O. in private audience. So, on 16th April I am to lunch with her at Windsor, and afterwards she will give me the Insignia without the usual formalities.

Warr had received the C.V.O. exactly thirty years earlier at the hands of her father in a similarly informal manner. In 1950, he had made Warr a K.C.V.O. The Victorian Order is given at the pleasure of the Sovereign for personal services, independent of the usual political channels through which bestowal of other British orders of chivalry is recommended. Charles had always greatly valued such tokens of his Sovereign's approval, but that the Grand Cross of the Order, a rare distinction, should be given him at Windsor in his last years by the Sovereign whom he had known since her childhood deeply touched him.

It is difficult to write anything about Charlie Warr without making him sound stuffy, because he was so Edwardian in his outlook and style. If you did not understand him, almost everything he said or did tended to come across with an air of stuffiness that was in fact entirely alien from his soul. I have never known anyone who could be so explosively merry in such a dignified way. I recall that when he was made an Honorary Fellow of the Royal College of Surgeons, I proposed, in jest of course, that I would gladly send him some patients. His laughter came out in a crescendo of chuckles and whoops. Only when they had died down and he had almost imperceptibly cleared his throat did he say with studied mock-seriousness, "I think I know some of the people you might have in mind." Rarely does one find a man of such self-conscious dignity of bearing and manner with such an uproarious sense of humor. It sprang from a combination of sensitiveness and openness of heart that became very endearing once you understood the man.

My last letter from Charles is dated April 24, 1969. I had told him I was coming to Britain that summer and would be preaching both in St. Paul's Cathedral, London, and in the seventeenth-century Canongate Kirk in Edinburgh that he attended in his retirement. He wrote:

I am so glad that we are going to meet again this summer, and especially glad that I am going to see you in the pulpit of the old Kirk of the Canongate . . . . The Queen is going to plant a tree in the approach to the Canongate Manse when she is here in May, so I hope it will be looking fresh to welcome you.

He concluded the two-page letter with, "All the best, and looking forward to seeing you in July." Alas, that meeting was never to take place. It happened that on the weekend of his death in Edinburgh I had been taken to hospital in Los Angeles for an appendectomy. A few days later I emplaned for London, since I had the engagement at St. Paul's Cathedral. Only when I had reached London did I hear the news of his death. On July 1, 1969, his secretary wrote me on behalf of his sister, Mrs. Turnbull:

Your letter has just come, much to our relief, as we knew you were not in Los Angeles and were anxious that you should not arrive in Edinburgh without having heard the sad news of Dr. Warr's death on 14th June . . . . He became acutely ill just before the Assembly and to his own bitter disappointment and that of all concerned he was not able to officiate at the Thistle Installation. The Queen sent him a charming letter in her own hand telling him how much she had missed him, but shortly after he had to go to a nursing home where the end came very suddenly after less than three weeks.

Dr. Warr wanted his memorial service to be very quiet and simple, and although the Queen and the Royal Family sent representatives, as well as nearly all the public bodies of Edinburgh, there was nothing formal about the gathering in the Canongate on 19th June since everyone there, in whatever capacity, was his friend.

Dr. Selby Wright, Dr. Warr's own minister since he retired, took the service most beautifully, assisted by Dr. Neville Davidson; and it would have made him so happy to see Roman Catholic and Anglican clergy sitting among members of the Edinburgh Presbytery, for it's generally admitted that the new and reconciling atmosphere of good will and mutual appreciation now spreading among the Churches in Scotland is due more to Dr. Warr than to any other man.

At the close of the service a piper from Dr. Warr's old regiment played a lament, and then the whole Canongate moved out to stand in the rain watching, while the long cortege drove away up the High Street to take him past St. Giles' for the last time. They had cleared the Mound of traffic and all the way down to the Crematorium policemen stood saluting at the crossings.

It was a wonderful farewell, and one that would greatly have astonished him; and yet we had the feeling that Edinburgh was not saying farewell at all but had gathered him up in its history.

Yours sincerely,
Hannah Aitken (Secretary)

What can one add to that unless it be the words spoken in the eulogy at his father's funeral? "Say not good-bye, but in some brighter clime bid me good morning." They are words echoed in Charles Warr's own novel, *The Call of the Island*, in which, in the midst of the carnage of Ypres, Lucile van den Zeele, her arms around her dying lover, whispers "low and tenderly," "Ivor, mon bien-aimé—ne disons pas adieu, mais au revoir!" Charles had a very deep sense of a world around us in another dimension that is beyond what we call life and death, a world where

Angel faces smile
Which I have loved long since, and lost a while.

THREE

Duncan MacGregor

Scotland was so Presbyterian at the time in which this chapter is set that people sometimes said in jest that even an atheist, if Scottish, would have to be a Presbyterian atheist. Scotland was almost as Presbyterian as Denmark had been Lutheran in the days when one of her most famous sons had said, in bitter satire, that one could not even open a bordello in Copenhagen without a baptismal certificate. The schisms that had so notoriously divided Scottish church life had been almost all within the Presbyterian framework. Moreover, the established Kirk, although less strikingly established than the Church of England, still played a notable part in the everyday life of the people. The rural parish minister was still at the center of local life, sometimes even serving it's medical and legal needs. If he were a man of any strength of character at all, as was often the case, he could command immense respect. He had been always well grounded, according to the standards of the day, in both humanities and biblical studies. Although no doubt few ministers could have been called scholars in any academic sense, they knew the meaning of scholarship. So a minister with scholarly ability and inclination could often find, in an obscure rural parish, opportunities to engage in scholarly pursuits that not even a university appointment in those leisurely days could have provided.

Duncan MacGregor (1854-1923) was not only a man of scholarly ability with diligence and zest to match, he was also totally devoid of worldly ambition. After a childhood and youth that did not seem to augur at all well for any sort of church vocation, he quickly settled down to the duties of his first and only parish, where he was to spend more than forty years, eventually dying "with his boots on." He learned to love and respect his people, the fisherfolk of northeast Scotland, and won from them devotion beyond price. The manse, as the minister's residence was called, became almost a throughway; yet his flock always respected, though they could not understand, his hours of scholarly seclusion. He married in 1880, a year before his ordination, and his wife bore him twelve children. He was a considerable poet, having published a long poem even in his undergraduate days at the University of Aberdeen and, soon after settling into parish life, a substantial little volume of poems. He had a gift for languages and a special interest in philology that he put to good use in his biblical and liturgical studies. Two of his hymns are still used in many churches to this day. During World War I, from his obscure parish, he did secret service work for the British War Office that one never heard him talk about. In all his life, the nearest he ever came to taking what would nowadays be called a sabbatical was a few months in the winter of 1900-1901, which he and his wife spent in Genoa, Italy.

Gneiss rocks?   *—Oh, very nice rocks.*

I first met my Uncle Duncan when I was a boy of nine, in February, 1919. It was a sad occasion for he had just received news of the death of his eldest daughter Theodora (Dora) in London, one of the many victims of the disastrous influenza epidemic. Dora, 37, at the time of her death, had been his favorite daughter. An Aberdeen graduate, she was the only one among all his children who fully shared his scholarly interests.

Despite his great personal sorrow at the time, his attitude of mind and outlook greatly intrigued me. I also liked his beard, which was then very much out of style. I had seen one or two beards but had never known anybody bearded to whom I could actually talk. I told him I hoped fairly soon to go to another school where I would learn science. He replied, "There is no such thing as science. There are sciences. You will learn sciences such as physics and chemistry."

Inevitably he inquired what I hoped to do when I grew up. I suggested various possibilities, with two predominating: tram conductor and prime minister. He listened seriously and then suggested that I might like to be a clergyman. A clergyman, when officiating, he said, is "higher than a king."

This, at the time, was too much for me to swallow. The only clergyman I knew at all well was a dwarfish man who wore a silk hat, day in, day out, over his disproportionately large head, as bald as an egg, giving him the look of Humpty-Dumpty in evening dress. His sermons were excruciatingly boring and very long. So I had never been much attracted to the cloth.

My uncle, however, was different. He took me for walks and as we went he always talked to me as though I were an adult, yet all the while imparting a bounteous cornucopia of information on the beauties of nature and on a variety of other subjects. I felt I learned more from him in half an hour than in a week at school.

It was on a later visit that he proposed my coming to his manse at Inverallochy and staying for the summer. He said I could easily make the train journey from Dundee alone. My mother's misgivings (I was only ten) were augmented by a threatened rail strike that might have left me stranded in Aberdeen, where I should have to change trains. He disposed of all such objections with manly disdain and I did indeed eventually take off.

I had been instructed that at Aberdeen I must go immediately to the other train which would take me to Fraserburgh, a distance of 46¾ miles that in those days on that line took a full three hours. There my aunt would be waiting for me. So much was the need for speed impressed upon me that on arrival in Aberdeen I leapt from the train and sped like a hare to the platform whence the other train was to leave. It was in fact already there but would not leave for nearly an hour. I asked four different fishwives whether this was indeed the right train. All replied in what might as well have been Cantonese, so far as my comprehension of their speech went.

In Fraserburgh likewise I plunged onto the station platform and rushed out so quickly that I completely eluded my aunt. Seeing no one I knew, and having diligently studied the map ahead of time, I walked the 3½ miles with my suitcase and, arriving at length in Inverallochy, I asked a huddle of village children for directions to the manse. They roared with laughter, partly at my speech but more at my ignorance. One of them beckoned another group, shouting "Here's a daft loonie fa disna ken faur the maunsse is!"

The manse was a solidly-built Victorian house with large bay windows in the two front downstairs rooms. It stood in a rectangular plot that served as flower and vegetable garden, and at that time it was the most important-looking dwelling in the village. Hence the local boys' amusement at my unheard-of ignorance. What, in their eyes, especially justified their derision was that I was standing square in front of it as I asked the question!

Paying not the slightest attention to their glee, I raced the hundred yards up the avenue (as the path through the manse garden was called, though there was not a tree in sight for miles in that flat Buchan countryside) to the door where I was welcomed with an astonishment that somehow gratified me.

It was in that house, in a musty book-lined study (my uncle's daily joy) that he pursued his scholarly researches. He carried his learning lightly, seeming to all appearance no more than a faithful rural minister. Not only was he an extraordinarily devoted pastor to his fisherfolk flock; he was a liturgical, philological and Celtic scholar. He was also a born poet, having had poems published in little magazines and local papers when he was only thirteen. When he was twenty and an Aberdeen undergraduate, he published *The Scald*, an extravaganza that went into two editions.

In one of his maturer poems he depicts his childhood love of nature and the songs his "virgin lips" once sang to her praise. Then he reflects:

I pity, as angel the woodland elf,
My former happy unhappy self.

In another he notes how old religious forms have given way, through the ages, to "Christian truth"; but he goes on to ask about the ways of his own generation:

Christian forms, are ye not also aging,
Swelling fruit in hardened kernels caging?

Yet he hankered after older Christian forms that he accounted richer. His Lee Lecture delivered in St. Giles', Edinburgh, on this theme, was published by Blackwood in 1895, to be followed by a tribute to St. Columba, published in 1897, the year of the thirteenth centenary of Columba's death, commemorated at the Abbey of Iona (then still in ruins) at a service in which he was the preacher. Among his numerous writings and contributions to both learned journals and popular magazines was an article in *The Scots Magazine* (September 1883), in which he offered a brief reconstruction of the ancient Scottish liturgy.

Uncle Duncan had been born on September 18, 1854 at Fort Augustus, where also his mother and his maternal grandparents had been born, the latter in the eighteenth century. His grandfather, William MacKinnon, a merchant there, had married Mary Grant of nearby Torranbreachd on February 20, 1821. I am fortunate to have inherited both their portraits, painted about 1835, and they now hang in the dining room of my California home.

They had ten children, every one of whom died in infancy except Jamesanna, who, born in 1828, lived to the age of 92, a petite lady with a formidable personality and highly literate tastes. She expected that her first child, if a boy, would become a clergyman, for that was fitting in her eyes for the first-born male as a thanksgiving to God. In her parents' family, since no male had survived, that ambition had been incapable of fulfillment.

Her father had been of a Jacobite family and her mother of a Hanoverian one: a "mixed marriage" in those days. William's own father had been such a perfervid Jacobite that on hearing of his son's intention to marry a Hanoverian, he refused to attend the wedding. He was later persuaded, by feminine guile, to do so and, of course, drank the health of the King over the water (I have never understood how they ever found water on a Highland table in those days).

On November 29, 1853, Duncan's mother, Jamesanna, married Alexander MacGregor, a parish schoolmaster, who within a few years was appointed to the Dunnichen parish school, near Forfar. Duncan's early years there did not look promising to a mother whose heart was set on giving a son to the Church. Duncan did not much like school and, in accordance with the universal practice of the age, was treated to abundant thrashings there at the hands of his father and, in the evenings, those of his mother (an even severer disciplinarian), in order to ensure the development of a greater devotion to school work.

For all that, he succeeded in being admitted to the University of Aberdeen at the age of 16.[1] More predictably, he was, according to all family testimony, such a wild undergraduate, such a resolute leader of scandalous student escapades, that he narrowly escaped being sent home. He participated, however, with great zest, not to say glee, in student literary and debating societies, from which he no doubt learned much.

Then at some point he suddenly matured into a very serious young man and gave himself up diligently to the studies required for the ministry of the Kirk. These included an emphasis on ancient languages, for which he had a natural instinct. At length he was licensed by the Presbytery of Aberdeen in 1877 and spent a few years serving missions at various places in the north, including Orkney and Gardenstown on the Banffshire coast, where he met his future wife, Anne Andrew. They were married on June 3, 1880. Between 1881 and 1902 she bore him twelve children.

Duncan was ordained by the Presbytery of Deer on December 15, 1881 and from then till his death on October 8, 1923 he served the parish of Inverallochy, the fishing village three and a half miles east of Fraserburgh. It was there, as a boy, that I came to know him so well during the summer holidays. I remember how he first broached the question with my mother on a visit to our home in Dundee. His excuse for luring me to the manse was twofold: (1) the sea air (which even in summer has a ferocious, sub-Arctic quality that either cures or kills) would do me good, which it certainly did, and (2) since his two youngest children were now grown up and off to the University of Aberdeen, the lack of a child in the house was intolerable.

I shall never forget the awe I experienced in seeing my Uncle Duncan perform his Sunday duties. He maintained till his last days the practice of reading alone in his study, the Old Testament lesson in Hebrew and the New Testament one in Greek, before the Sunday service. At the first stroke of the bell he would leave his study and walk to the church at the end of the manse garden path, where the smell of mint was heavy. Despite his natural propensity for laughter and fun (he never lost a boyish delight in perpetrating harmless practical jokes), he always made that procession of one with the gravity of gait and mien befitting a Guards' parade.

As he entered the arched doorway at the side of the church, wearing a simple black gown, his eyes lowered and his countenance aglow as if with reverence for the work he was about to undertake, a hush swept through the congregation of bronze-faced fisherfolk. He advanced in solitary reverence to the pulpit. From the manse pew could be seen just a white streak of his clerical collar, all but hidden by his ample, black, slightly greying beard as he bowed his head in silent prayer for a few ticks of the large, friendly-faced clock under the gallery. Then, after the great opening words, "Let us worship God," would rise the tremendous roar of eager, fresh voices, of every age and timbre:

God is our refuge and our strength, in straits a present aid;
Therefore, although the earth remove, we will not be afraid:
Though hills amidst the seas be cast; Though waters roaring make,
And troubled be; yea, though the hills by swelling seas do shake.

For a people often exposed to the howling winds of the North Sea, where the men were out at sea in every kind of weather, it was as much a hymn of thanksgiving for a week of safe returns as it was what liturgists would have called it, a psalm of praise.

Outside the pulpit, Uncle Duncan had a quick tongue. Asked by a visiting clergyman why he went to such trouble preparing to preach to such simple folk as though they were learned scholars, when, presumably, it could make no difference to them, he replied unhesitatingly, "On the contrary, if my people were learned what I said would not matter so much. They could test it for themselves. It is because they are such simple folk that it is my special duty not to mislead them." He often reminded me that his flock followed the same trade as the first disciples.

He was as devoid of prejudice about people as anyone I have ever known. He moved with the greatest of ease among all classes, rich or poor, noble or peasant. The only fierce antipathy I ever found in him was against anyone he took to be pretentious or arrogant. A house guest, a university professor of geology, once came into this category.

Duncan, with his flair for practical jokes, took him for a walk along the shore, and waved towards some rocks.

"Nice rocks," he remarked innocently.

"Oh, very nice rocks," cooed the geologist patronizingly.

"I mean, of course, G-N-E-I-S-S rocks," spelling out the letters gleefully.

Perhaps it was Duncan's combination of unworldliness (he had almost no business sense at all) and love of people, especially simple people like his fisherfolk, that made him such a beloved pastor. The manse was too hospitable, almost a public thoroughfare. Parishioners habitually came in at the front door and emerged from the back.

When typhoid fever struck the region, Duncan moved from one afflicted house to another not only with ministrations of Christian grace but with both medical and legal counsel which he was remarkably fitted to provide, having been for long doctor and lawyer as well as minister to his beloved people. Of course in the end he came down with typhoid himself. He expected that. He came staggering into his manse late one night, grievously ill after a long day of pastoral visitation of the victims. Unlike many of them, he recovered.

One wonders how anyone survived. There was no running water as we understand it today, except from the village pump, which in summer often ran dry, and at the foot of the manse garden, where we left a huge tub all night, in hope that the feeble pressure would come on during the night for an hour or so and fill it. In the morning it was usually filled, with a thin layer of insects on top, which were simply skimmed off and the water then boiled on the paraffin stove—a ceremony that was often only perfunctorily performed.

The dry toilet at the end of the garden near the church was a bucket that was periodically emptied for use as fertilizer, hence the abundant cultivation of mint in its vicinity, without which nobody with a vestige of olfactory sensibility could have withstood a visit thither. My uncle, by the way, for all the sharpness of his eyes and ears, was bereft of a sense of smell, a fact that some perceptive readers of his poems have detected.

With a poultry yard and a well-stocked vegetable garden there was always plenty of good plain food on the manse table, even for so large a family. Much less easily satisfied was my uncle's voracious appetite for books. His large library never appeased it. Aberdeen was accounted a long journey; certainly one could not have zoomed thither and back to look up a reference as some might do today.

I have a vivid image of him at the age of sixty-five with an hour to spare in Dundee en route for home and his customary gnawing hunger for books. A few hundred yards from the Tay Bridge Station was the open-air Greenmarket where on Saturdays was displayed (besides much else) a vast array of books for sale, many of them scholarly and all of them priced between a penny and a sixpence. Somewhere my uncle found a huge jute sack and, arrayed as always in full clerical dress with wide black hat (well, greenish-black), began buying books galore and stuffing them into the sack. By the time his last shilling was gone the sack was so heavy he had to drag it along the cobbled streets and down the steps of the station, gloating over his treasure as though he were carrying off gold bullion from the Mint.

What anyone thought of him was to Duncan a matter of total unconcern. Soon he would be trying the impossible feat of heaving it onto the train and of course a strong man would rush to his assistance and receive his priceless blessing. I could not help, for my arms were laden with volumes he had bought and thrust upon me. I still own one of them—Smith's *Latin-English Dictionary*, 1857, a reliable work. Greenmarket price: one penny.

In the manse library, inconspicuous in a cheap rexine cover on one of the lower shelves opposite the window, was a treasure that not only would have commanded an enormous price at any big book auction today but was also of unique historical and scholarly importance. In my summers at the manse I chanced upon it while my uncle was reading in his chair, as he did almost constantly in the last years of his life when I knew him best. I took it out from the shelf and began perusing it. By that time I had begun the study of Latin and could make out some phrases. My uncle suddenly looked up, with a slightly startled stare, asking if I knew what it was. I remarked on the "paper", which was vellum. He gave me a long talk on the nature of the book, explaining that it was a 15th century medieval manuscript, a manual for priests' use in performing various offices such as marriages and funerals, and for various kinds of blessing. I was enthralled. He told me to look at it as much as I pleased but to be sure to put it back in its place, which of course I did. When I went back the following year, the last of my three summers at the manse, I sought it, studied it even more diligently with my now better Latin, and again carefully replaced it.

Manuscripts of this sort, containing liturgical texts of Scottish provenance, are comparatively rare. This one had been discovered in the library of a neighboring minister, Dr. John F.M. Cock, the incumbent of the parish of Rathen. On Dr. Cock's death his representatives, knowing of my uncle's abilities in such matters, generously passed the manuscript into his possession and ownership. My uncle had edited and translated it and much of his work was published with his notes by the Aberdeen Ecclesiological Society in 1905. It is known to scholars as the *The Rathen Manual*.

When my uncle died in 1923, one of his sons, an Edinburgh lawyer, wrote me (I was then 13, almost 14) to say that the manuscript could not be found. Had I seen it? If so, could I give him a description? I replied with a description in considerable detail, which I now know to have been remarkably accurate, since it corresponded closely to that given in the edited version and translated in the published account, of which I was then of course entirely ignorant. The principal information I was able to provide beyond what was available to scholars, thanks to my uncle's editing and publication, was about the rexine cover and the location of the manuscript in his library.

In now more than 60 years no trace of it has been found. One theory put forward was that he might have lent it to a monk of the Benedictine Abbey at Fort Augustus with whom he was on friendly terms. My own feeling is that at his death his books were taken to a bookseller's in Fraserburgh who saw only an untidy volume in a cheap cover and consigned it with other "rubbish" to the flames.

I have only one of my uncle's letters. Dated January 31, 1901, it bears the unlikeliest of addresses: Via Palestro 5, Genoa. In the 42 years of his incumbency he was rarely out of his parish and never for more than a few weeks except for this one six-month leave around the turn of the century. He spent most of it in Italy. Eight pages long, the letter is full of his excitement over the wonders he has seen and the interesting people he has met: Franciscan priests, Waldensian pastors, and the Marchese di Grupallo.

He described how he dropped in to a preaching marathon at an evening mission, at which one monk preached hell and damnation till the people wept in terror, to be followed by another who kept tham laughing all through the next sermon. He remarked on the music "an orchestra, chiefly violins" and on the illumination: "no theatre could compete with it in splendour." He described also the gardens of the Marchese's palazzo, adding the tragic note that, alas, the Marchese could not enjoy them: he was blind.

Imagine the excitement of this once-in-a-lifetime odyssey for him and his beloved Anne! En route for Italy he stopped for a haircut while he was in Paris. According to a family tradition the Parisian barber gasped with horror at the vastness of his beard and said, 'Ah, Révérend Père, vous êtes revenu d'une des missions africaines?'[2]

Although above all else a scholarly churchman, Duncan also felt deep loyalty to King and country. Only after his death did I learn how secret had been his patriotic contribution. Almost sixty at the outbreak of World War I in 1914, he was obviously beyond active military service, but he volunteered for work with British Intelligence. His eldest son, Alpin, while serving with the Gordon Highlanders in front-line combat, was captured and taken to a German prison camp.

Duncan conducted a secret and very dangerous correspondence with him in code, which sometimes yielded information of considerable value to the War Office. He sometimes conducted his part by sending his son inquiries on tiny slips of paper tucked into the middle of a jar of jam or other goody such as fathers sent their sons to cheer them in camp. On one occasion the camp commandant suddenly announced that he had reason to believe that important military information was leaking from the camp and he was about to make a formal search. Anyone whose belongings turned up incriminating evidence would be shot. Alpin quaked, for a jar of marmalade had just arrived and he had not had time to open it let alone swallow the telltale slip. As the commandant reached Alpin, however, he murmured to his aides something to the effect, "Skip him—he's the only one in the camp I can trust." Duncan's prayers for his son must surely have been working well.

It was always difficult to discern, in his multifaceted personality, which was the real Duncan; but I think we could not go far wrong in seeing it in a poem of his that was his own favorite:

WANTED

Wanted: Men.
Not systems fit and wise,
Not faiths with rigid eyes,
Not wealth in mountain piles,
Not power with gracious smiles,
Not even the potent pen;
Wanted: Men.

Wanted: Deeds.
Not words of winning note,
Not thoughts fom life remote,
Not fond religious airs,
Not sweetly languid prayers,
Not love of sects and creeds;
Wanted: Deeds.

Men and Deeds.
Men that can dare and do,
Not longings for the new,
Not pratings of the old,
Good life and actions bold—
These the occasion needs:
Men and Deeds.

In his last years, unfortunately, ill health overtook him. He was a diabetic and also suffered a stroke. He used to roar with laughter as he recounted that what the doctors prescribed for the one contradicted the treatment for the other. At least it was a good story and Duncan loved nothing better than that, God and Nature excepted. When he died in 1923, his estate was valued at just under 81 pounds sterling. Unbusinesslike to the end, he left no will.

Twelve years after his death I revisited Inverallochy. Walking along the sugar-white Buchan sands I found some fisherfolk working at their nets. By this time I was a grown man. I engaged one sunbeaten old fisherman in conversation. Did he by any chance remember the Reverend Duncan MacGregor? He glanced up at me, indifference suddenly giving way to zest.

"MacGreegor? Aye I mind him fine. A *great* man."

"And a *good* man," chimed in another, looking up from his nets.

"The *best*," added a third with that chilled emotion that is all the local code of conduct would permit.

"Ee ken, thae lads i' the Kirk, they gangs tae coalleges, ee ken, an' their heids *expaunds*."[3]

"Aye," chimed a growing chorus.

There was a long, meditative silence. Then someone spoke up more sharply. "MacGreegor was special. Verr-r-ry special. Everybody respeckit him. Aye they respeckit him for what he was, for what he was."

Again a pause and an old woman murmured, "His wife didna help him, maybe, the wye she micht. Och, she meant weel, ee ken, but she was a wee bittie ower glib o' the tongue." Perhaps the old woman had forgotten the dozen children the Lady of the Manse had brought into the world and nurtured and fed and clothed. Perhaps, too, the woman had forgotten her services as organist. Duncan's wife was very musical.

"He worked *wonders*," remarked another woman pointedly, ignoring the slight denigration of the Lady of the Manse with just a *soupcon* of a hint that it was to be attributed to feminine jealousy.

This time the pause was so long that a fisherman ostentatiously cleared his throat as if duty were enforcing speech. "Aye," he said awkwardly. "He was *respeckit* a' richt. Even—even the *coos* respeckit him."

The notion that the cows could also pay their homage reduced everybody, including myself, to laughter. But in the deep, thoughtful silence that ensued I looked out at the giant waves gleaming in the northern sunlight and somehow I could hear them utter the words the fisherfolk meant deep down in their hearts, words they could not have spoken, words they had so often heard from the pulpit:

"What manner of man is this, that even the winds and the sea obey him?"

Austin Farrer

Duncan MacGregor & his wife Anne

A. D. Ritchie

FOUR

Austin Farrer

Austin Farrer (1904-1969) received his education at St. Paul's School, London, and at Balliol College, Oxford, where his brilliance was rewarded with a triple first class degree. Ordained Anglican priest in 1929, he served in a Yorkshire parish for a few years, then as Chaplain and Tutor, St. Edmund Hall, Oxford, till 1935, when he became Fellow and Chaplain of Trinity College, Oxford. He remained there till 1960, when he accepted appointment as Warden of Keble College, Oxford. He died suddenly in the middle of the night on February 20, in his mid-sixties.

A genius of the first order, Farrer was intellectually unique in his combination of extraordinarily quick analytical powers and (which he valued much more) original creative insight and boldness in his use of it. He was a prolific author. His writings, at first difficult because of an elliptical style, became more and more delightfully readable, his immense learning shining through every paragraph yet elegantly concealed under a masterly beautiful simplicity of style. With a Leonardesque ability to turn from one field of expertise to another, he startled more staid colleagues by seeming to intrude on scholarly terrain they accounted their preserve. Some of them, imprisoned in an academic specialization, treated him as if guilty of trespass. Farrer, however, cared little where his fertile mind alighted, so long as it was bent, as it always was, in pursuit of truth.

He was, from his undergraduate days, a convinced Anglo-Catholic. His shy manner concealed an immense mental strength but could not disguise the sparkling wit that was the fruit of a lightning-like mind. Remaining for many years closely tied to Oxford, he later went farther afield, giving, for example, the Terry Lectures at Yale and the Gifford Lectures at Edinburgh. He was made an Honorary Fellow of Trinity in 1963 and a Fellow of the British Academy in 1968. There is an entry for him in the *Dictionary of National Biography*.

He was rather as though a flash of lightning had somehow been trapped in a slender papyrus reed and was just about to break loose.

Some forty years ago, when I first saw a notice of my proposed D.Phil. thesis topic in the *Oxford University Gazette,* I was much dismayed to find the name of A. M. Farrer of Trinity listed as the supervisor the University had appointed. I had hoped to do my work, which was on the function of aesthetic experience in religion,[1] under a Fellow of my own college (Queen's) who, however, had meanwhile accepted a professorial chair at Cambridge. Farrer's name at that time was entirely unknown to me and little known beyond a few of his intimate friends at Oxford. He had published no books, although his first and most difficult book, *Finite and Infinite,* was about to make its appearance. True, he was, as I quickly ascertained, a young Fellow of Trinity who had taken a triple first (Mods 1925, Greats 1927, and Theology 1928), but such academic laurels are not in themselves by any means reassuring to a doctoral candidate. Triple firsts can be tiresome eccentrics or arrogant upstarts or both, not least when, as in his case, they are only five years one's senior. I felt at worst cheated, at best apprehensive.

Although it was to be some time before I could know the full measure of my singular good fortune, I quickly perceived at least that I had fallen in with an extraordinary young genius. Austin Farrer was the nearest thing to pure spirit that one is likely ever to see in a human embodiment. Sometimes I wondered, indeed, whether I were talking to a man or encountering an angel lightly disguised. For Farrer's presence was like that of a bright flame. He was as perhaps one might imagine one of the "separate intelligences" in the Thomistic angelology.

Farrer's fair hair, blue eyes, and slim figure all contributed to the ethereality of his presence; but one was hardly aware of them as he talked. Neither his smile (a mixture of boyish mischief and shy kindliness) nor his frown (a momentary manifestation of passing pain) seemed to have any particular shape or visible contour that could catch an artist's eye. They were more like rapid alternations in the stream of flame that was his presence: lightenings and darkenings that darted straight into one's consciousness without the usual interpretative process. Nor was one aware of his height, which was middling, but only of the white clerical collar that girded the flame.

He first manifested himself to me in the form of a brief letter in his distinctive, old-fashioned English hand. It was to the effect that while he was not sure whether it were he who should make the first move, he would make bold to wonder whether I might care to take tea with him on a certain afternoon at his home.

At the appointed hour I duly appeared, of course, at the door of his modest dwelling, where a rather clumsy daily help attempted to deal with me but was intercepted at once by an excited Mrs. Farrer crying shrilly, "No, no, no, I'll cope." I was then ushered quickly into the living room where Farrer, who happened to be in a standing position, physically withdrew several steps at my approach as though he feared for his life at the advance of a possibly wild creature that had descended upon him from the wilderness of the outside world. (Farrer often gave the impression of a stage caricature of donnish Englishness.) The retreat was due to pure shyness, a byproduct of an almost schoolboy awkwardness conjoined to a scintillating intellect and (though much more heavily disguised) an intense poetic sensitivity.

He was charming in no conventional sense. Indeed, some of my contemporaries openly laughed when I hinted that Austin Farrer had charm. Yet he certainly had, if only one did not come with a prejudiced view of what charm has to be. At any rate, I instinctively perceived that I was in the presence of someone most unusual.

After a few sips of tea and some civilities in which his awkwardness was at its height, he somewhat coyly alluded to the work I was proposing. I described as succinctly as I could what I had in mind and politely asked what he thought of it.

Nodding and smiling evasively as I spoke, he replied at length with a slight fidget, "Ye-es, of course. It is just that I am so ignorant of the subject." He always spoke with an exactness that would have sounded formal, even pedantic, but for the pervading lyrical quality that gave almost all his utterances the cadences of a quietly joyful liturgical hymn. Only an oaf could have taken seriously his protestations of ignorance. Within a few minutes his erudition was inconspicuously and parenthetically pouring out on the fringes of the creativity and originality of his ever restless mind.

His first tokens of encouragement were plainly superficial. For several weeks I could extract little criticism and less praise. Only slight noises passed his lips, mostly sounding "mm-mm! mm-mm?ym-mm! ym-mm? nm-mm!" I could interpret these politely nondiscursive remarks as I pleased, but even on the most optimistic view they could hardly be taken as other than expressions of courteously concealed boredom tinged with a deep despair alternating with minute *soupçons* of hope. Occasionally he would gently hint that I might be engaged in an encyclopedia rather than sustaining a thesis: a common misadventure among doctoral aspirants. Yet at times I was able to convince myself that the pained looks were growing less frequent and that behind the old-fashioned gold-rimmed spectacles a warmer glow was beginning to make its appearance in his eyes.

About this time I noticed in a university announcement that Farrer was giving a series of public lectures. I attended. They were disasters. He walked awkwardly up and down the room like a deer at a cattle market. The audience was sparse, with an unwelcome representation of the eccentrics that tend to haunt theological lectures. He talked jerkily and often as though to himself and the angels. As often as not he looked out the window with a faraway smile on his lips. His style was extremely difficult to follow in those days. Yet he never failed to convey to me the impression that he had just emerged from heaven, having too little experience of addressing flesh-clad mortals and no knowledge of how to slow down the fire of his mind in such a way as to keep the dross of our bodies from inadvertently extinguishing it. At times, however, I felt I was suddenly able to apprehend; then a moment later no less suddenly was I harboring doubts.

One day, keeping an appointment with him, I entered his room at Trinity and sat down as usual. I had written a paper for him on Croce and waited to hear what he thought of it. In his quietly elegant way and as though speaking polyphonically in Greek and Latin with English as a mere lively descant upon them, "I have read you with singular pleasure!" He then went on to specify the nature of it: I had stimulated a new train of thought in his mind on the subject of aesthetic experience. He did mention that Croce was not within the ambit of his own accustomed thought patterns, but he then went on to specify with sharp precision the nature of his appreciation of my interpretation of the Italian neoidealist and compared it with the work of R. G. Collingwood, who had just gone from the earthly scene. The openness with which Farrer was willing to inspect thought that was at once unfashionable among British philosophers, alien to the scholastic theological tradition in which he was working at the time, and outside his own personal interests, deeply impressed me.

So reticent was he about his own personal interests that only by my third term with him did I either grasp the nature of his poetic genius or even recognize how deeply Catholic was the temper of his personal churchmanship. By this time *Finite and Infinite* had appeared and had puzzled most of us who tried to read it. A long review of it by Eric Mascall helped to elucidate it, but no one could have called it easy reading. Austin had at that time an elliptical style, very different from that of his later writings and posthumously published sermons and addresses. In his earlier days, he tended to assume in his readers not only an erudition but a perceptivity such as his own. Yet, though I knew so little about him in those early days, I never once left his presence without feeling as though angels' wings had brushed past me. One day, as we finished an hour of talk about my work, I was about to take my leave when he inquired shyly, "Would you—would you like to see my new toy?"

His new toy turned out to be his incipient work on New Testament studies which, when published, was seen to be highly original but extremely controversial. Running counter to the already widely accepted views of New Testament scholars in Europe and America, it could not but have been destined to evoke the academic hostility it inevitably engendered. Farrer behaved as though he fully expected a hostile reception. The prospect had not the slightest effect on him.

I listened intently. The speed and lightness of his exposition reminded me of how a nimble-fingered pianist can make Chopin sound easy to play. The customary enigmatic smile came at last, with a built-in, unspoken interrogation. He was inviting criticism. I offered the first that came into my head. Was not the extremely elaborate and complex arrangement of symbols by which he was proposing to interpret the thought of New Testament writers far beyond their capacity? Did not it read into their thought much more than could have been there? Is not one of the commonest errors we make in interpreting the thought of ancient peoples the fastening upon them of subtleties and distinctions that come naturally to us but must have been beyond them?

He glowed with delight, for the underlying purpose of his "new toy" was indeed to show that New Testament scholars had reached their basic conclusions by doing something of that sort. Nevertheless, he denied that the objection applied to what he was doing.

"They were not at all simplistic *in that way*," he said firmly. "May it be that you have fallen prey to the error of supposing that because the New Testament writers knew nothing about telephones and typewriters they were equally ignorant in all else? In the use and arrangement of symbols they were in fact much subtler than we." Austin's manner of speaking would have been pedantic had he employed the heavy diction pedants commonly use, but he spoke with such elegant lightness that everything he said sounded colloquial, angelic though his colloquy seemed.

On a subsequent occasion of the same kind I had come to perceive that, on the theory he was proposing about the writing of the Gospels, he had no need of the hypothesis of Kirsopp Lake and others, which had become universally accepted by New Testament scholars, that the Synoptists (Matthew, Mark, Luke) had worked from a common source. The hypothetical source is designated Q.

"Q is the rankest red herring ever drawn across the path of truth," he affirmed quietly as if he were telling an elementary chemistry class that the boiling point of water is 100 degrees centigrade.

The confidence of his disposal of Q shocked me. Like all theological students I had been trained to accept Q as beyond question. I had found it convincing and still do. Yet that this young, lone, donnish Oxford scholar should set out in a discipline other than his own, follow his own hunch, carefully work out his arguments, and without a vestige of arrogance boldly propose it to the world, struck me as a most refreshing find in the groves of academe. For despite the openness of mind we rightly expect to find in scholars today, there is, in fact, more reliance than most would readily admit on tradition and professional authority. Innovators are not publicly treated as heretics, fit for burning at the stake; but they do face hostility and formidable obstacles, often in unexpected places. Moreover, scholars today are notoriously and perhaps increasingly jealous of their own academic disciplines. They resent intrusion by even the most distinguished of outsiders. Such is the accepted classification of disciplines within broad academic fields that, to a New Testament scholar, a philosophical theologian such as Farrer is almost as much of an outsider as would be an art historian or a chemist. (Much the same happens in the fields of medicine and law.) The Q hypothesis remains widely sacrosanct; nevertheless, Farrer's writings, especially *A Study in Mark*, have at least reminded us all that even the most convincing of hypotheses is not inviolable.

In 1937, Austin had married Katharine Newton, an Oxford graduate and a gifted and accomplished lady. Katharine seemed to fit the scenery of the Farrer household with an almost computer-like inevitability. She translated Gabriel Marcel's *Etre et avoir* and wrote some novels. One tended to get the impression that if one could but eavesdrop on their intimate conversation at, say, breakfast or bedtime, when most of us would be discussing perhaps the events of the day or plans for a weekend at cousin Bette's, the Farrers would be more likely to be talking of the extent of Pythagorean influence on Dante and Austin would be finding relaxation in such light conversation.

In fact, upholstery and gardening were prominent among Austin's hobbies. Katharine was, however, of an unfortunately highly-strung and nervous disposition. The only other member of the family I had encountered in my early acquaintance with the Farrer household was an elderly aunt who seemed to be made of porcelain and added to the general impression of ethereality. Katharine was also strikingly and, at times, almost unbelievably insular in her Englishness. Many years later, after I had settled in the United States, she would say things like, "Americans are awfully good with horses, aren't they?" and Austin would look momentarily pained as though a talkative child had asked about Aunt Matilda's wooden leg.

One day while Austin Farrer and I were discussing something very philosophical at his home, a little girl burst into the room and ran across it noisily before Katharine could rush in and escort her quickly out of it. In the course of this episode Farrer looked momentarily more sad than pained. The little girl was their only child. Her mind had not developed beyond about the age of two: a peculiarly poignant tragedy in such a household. At the time I still knew nothing of it. In reading Austin's modest little book on the philosophical problem of evil, *Love Almighty and Ills Unlimited*, one should bear in mind how much more lies behind that exposition of a Christian stance on a classic subject than the philosophical and theological arguments set forth across its pages. But then to anyone who really knew Austin, there is always so very much more behind his utterances than was ever uttered.

He tried but was not really very good at suffering fools gladly. I once attended a discussion (the Socratic Club, I think it was) at which he was to cross swords with a young scientist on the subject of religion. The scientist was far from being an original or creative mind in scientific thought or anything else. His attacks on religion were so ill-informed that almost any educated Christian might well have felt that Christian charity demanded that one try to help him do a better job. Yet he plowed on relentlessly, seemingly quite ignorant of how jejune he seemed to so many in his audience. It was truly a battle between a bull and the matador, although in this case the bull really thought it was he who had killed the man. Next day Farrer, having detected my presence at the discussion, although I had been silent throughout it, greeted me, "Well, that *was* fourth-form!"[2] He never said another word about the evening's debate.

Although Farrer found the sophomoric mildly amusing, ponderous language of any kind tended to evoke an audible sigh. He came in slightly late for my appointment with him one afternoon, explaining that he had had to be a witness in court on behalf of an undergraduate who had fallen foul of the law.

"Oh dear," he sighed. "Such *heavy* language! What would they say of us were *we* to talk like that?" Only a faint smile was visible and that but fleetingly. No doubt he had been not only bored but annoyed at such a waste of time that could have been devoted to more intellectually profitable pursuits, such as, say, the philosophy of the imagination. Perhaps he chose to ignore that philosophers and theologians can be as ponderous as any lawyer. Few indeed have anything like his eloquent lightness of touch.

When I was first in England after he had gone from Trinity to Keble, I telephoned him, announcing that my wife and I were briefly in Oxford. Might we call on him? He offered me a choice: to take tea or to come later for sherry. Making some reference to the freedom of the will (in allusion to his book, *The Freedom of the Will*, published in 1958), I could hear the merest whisper of a chuckle before I chose tea.

Austin's friends would have preferred to have seen him elected to an Oxford chair of theology rather than to a college headship, however prestigious, and surely no one could have better adorned a theological chair. Austin seemed not to have wished to be considered for the Nolloth Chair, which carries a fellowship at Oriel College; but he would have welcomed appointment to the Regius Chair of Divinity at Christ Church. The general expectation was that it would go to him when it fell vacant. However, mysterious are the ways of academe. He was overlooked, to his wife's intense and undisguised indignation.

He would have been a uniquely felicitous choice. No doubt he was disappointed. An Oxford tutor, not least one so conscientious in his teaching duties, wearies of decades of tutoring and cannot but hanker after the greater freedom that a professorial chair at Oxford can afford.

Farrer must have seemed to many an unlikely type for a twentieth-century college administrator. Yet not only did he turn to the business of running a college with the zest and sharpness of mind that he brought to everything else he did; his administrative responsibilities did nothing to diminish the steady literary flow of the last decade of his life.

At the entrance to the Warden's Lodging that afternoon of our visit, we were about to proceed up the long flight of stairs when a shrill cry came from on high. "Ah, come up and behold it—and all the glory thereof." Austin never said anything in prose if there were any decent way of saying it in poetry. Then soon he was wandering around with a large kettle that seemed to dangle from a flexible wrist. He either talked or looked pained while Katharine blurted out one of her celebrated pronouncements on America, as though it were one of the remoter provinces of Antarctica that modern technology had recently made almost habitable. But before the end of the visit he had spirited my wife away for a moment to tell her how well he had always thought of me and of my work. Indeed it had been his chance recommendation in answer to a query from Bryn Mawr that had been mainly instrumental in my appointment there in 1949. I did not know that at the time; I discovered it years later.

Farrer's perception of the United States was much more realistic than that of his wife. Nevertheless, when he gave the Terry Lectures at Yale he was somewhat alarmed to discover that his book that contained the text of the lectures had already been published. He told me he feared the audience might arrive, each with book in hand, demanding to know in what particular his lectures could be said to advance beyond the book they had just read. Alas, in America as elsewhere, neither books nor lectures are nowadays taken quite so seriously as once they were.

It happened that I was going to New York on business at the time he was preaching in the Cathedral of St. John the Divine, so I went of course to hear him. The idea of Farrer in that enormous and somewhat overpowering building (longer than any English cathedral, even Winchester or St. Alban's, and immensely impressive) intrigued me. Nor was I disappointed as his slim surpliced figure minced its way across the Great Quire and up the steps of the pulpit like a benign spirit wending its heavenward path. He seemed straight out of the Apocalypse to whose author that great church is dedicated.

Somehow he was incongruous with his surroundings whenever these were more than a few miles out of Oxford. But then everything about Austin Farrer was incongruous with his circumstances. For instance, that he was the son of a prominent Baptist was almost as unexpected as if Thérèse de Lisieux had been the daughter of a Russian rabbi.

"They never told me," he began with the kind of firm simplicity that Newman's contemporaries attributed to his style of preaching, "that the nightingale could be heard in Central Park." The sermon was on the problem of evil and preached with quiet, masterly skill, but a more unlikely opening could hardly have been imagined. Perhaps he was the only person in the cathedral who had paid so much attention to the sound of nightingales in the park.

Farrer's extraordinary genius for stripping a philosophical problem down to its essence made him mildly impatient of the fashionable preoccupation with analytical detail that, by my time, had gripped Oxford. Moreover, his astonishing array of other gifts obscured to some people his singularly keen philosophical acumen. His father's form of Christianity seemed to have left no mark on him at all, positive or negative. In his early youth, he had been fascinated by Spinoza (a well-known sign of metaphysical acuity) and it was really, I suspect, through Spinozism that he found his way to Anglo-Catholicism, to which he remained devoted and within which he exercised his intellectual talents. Although he greatly admired Aristotle he was, I believe, a Platonist at heart, as indeed, of course, was St. Thomas. More than once, he expressed to me rather pointedly his affection for the early Christian School of Alexandria, whose exponents were Christian Platonists or, as some would say, Christian Gnostics. That *genre* of Christian thought would have appealed to one who, perhaps, had never entirely lost his early fascination for Spinoza.

Farrer always seemed attentive to criticism of any kind but quite impervious to any of it that he found ineffective. One of the most formidable critics of his New Testament work was Helen Gardner, a notable English literary scholar whom many universities delighted to honor. They were in many ways poles apart and it is not easy to imagine how there could ever have been genuine understanding between them. Their dialogue was attended by coldly polite acrimony. Yet when I talked with Dame Helen at luncheon in a friend's house in Malibu, California, some years after Farrer's death, and suggested that, whatever one thought of his ingenious speculations on the New Testament, he was indeed a saint and a saint of a special kind, she not only conceded this but applauded it. It would have been difficult indeed for anyone to deny that, if there is another and higher dimension of being, Farrer, of all people, must surely belong to it.

My own experience of him was, however, more special than that. I did not merely "get to know him." From the moment I first met him I felt as though I had always known him. He unfolded himself gradually and in such a way that I always felt as though there had never been a time when I did not know him at all. After I left Oxford, we conducted a long, almost constant correspondence over the course of more than twenty years, always in his distinctive, old-fashioned hand and each letter containing something lively and often novel. I often wanted to say how much I cherished his friendship, but it was difficult because he seemed to be always burning only for truth about God. Anything not so definitely focused sounded therefore banal. Yet all the while, what he was saying sounded so natural. I felt as though from time immemorial, I had witnessed his awesome strength of mind cooped up in a fragile body. Yet to say that his body seemed fragile is misleading, for his presence conveyed an impression of immense strength. He was rather as though a flash of lightning had somehow been trapped in a slender papyrus reed and was just about to break loose. Nothing fragile about that.

As I think of Farrer today, the image that comes most readily to mind is of him riding a bicycle along the Broad. I see him as a slim, black figure perched on a machine that seems to have no relation to its rider but to which he is somehow precariously attached as it transports him along like a parcel it has been computerized to carry. I see him whiz by, looking neither at me nor at anyone else but smiling tolerantly at Oxford and the world, perhaps especially at Oxford.

News of his very sudden death came to me as a grievous shock. Then all at once I felt how natural it seemed for Austin to have slipped away from the earthiness of this life. I began to marvel more that it had not happened sooner. Most of all I marvelled at my singular good fortune in having for so long known so nimble an intellect companying so constantly close to God as he sped swiftly across the path of this our mortal life.

FIVE

Arthur David Ritchie

Arthur David Ritchie (1891-1967) was the son of D. G. Ritchie, a professor of philosophy at St. Andrews University whose work on natural rights was well known. Only eight when his father died, David was an only son, much cherished and protected. His inclination towards the sciences was evident in early childhood, when he began a collection of wildflowers that he preserved, dated, and classified, and to which he continued to add special finds much later in life.

He entered Fettes College, Edinburgh, but was forced to leave after a year due to ill health. It was probably there, however, that he developed his interest in Chemistry. He continued his studies at home, and, when his mother moved south and built a house on the Devon coast, a lab was built for David alongside his study. His circumstances there encouraged him in an interest in marine biology and he learned sailing to help in his pursuit of it. He finished his education at Trinity College, Cambridge, where, after World War I, he became a Fellow.

During the war, the University of Manchester supplied a panel of scholars and scientists to go at short notice to British and American air bases and elsewhere to lead discussion groups and answer questions. Ritchie was one of the stars of the panel, quoting from a wide variety of sources beyond his own scientific and philosophical interests. His wide range of knowledge coupled with the lightness of his touch made him quite popular. The war years reinforced his frugal habits as he lived with other scientists, for security reasons, in rough quarters in the Essex marshes.

In 1926, he left his fellowship at Cambridge to join a team of scientists at the University of Manchester working on the chemical aspect of muscle physiology. While holding various positions in the medical school, he came under the influence of Samuel Alexander, a noted British philosopher, and turned more and more toward philosophical studies. Alexander, who had been a contemporary and friend of Ritchie's father at Oxford, was succeeded in his Manchester chair by John Stocks. When the latter left to become Vice-Chancellor of the University of Liverpool in 1937, Ritchie was invited to occupy that chair. He remained there till 1945, when he succeeded Norman Kemp Smith, the doyen of British philosophers in his day, in the chair of Logic and Metaphysics at the University of Edinburgh.

In the late forties, to which this chapter relates, the University of Edinburgh was internationally known and often attracted notable professors. For a philosopher of Scottish birth and ancestry to follow Kemp Smith at Edinburgh was considered the attainment of the pinnacle of his career. It might have turned another man's head. To those who knew Ritchie, whose quiet modesty was so extreme as to be almost a fault, the notion that anything could ever turn his head seems quite laughable.

Scotland was home to him but Cambridge had moulded his mind.

The Scottish system of higher education, in the mid-twentieth century, consisted of four universities, all ancient. Each was independent, yet all stood together, sharply distinguished from the twelve English universities, which consisted of Oxford and Cambridge on the one hand, and on the other, London and the provincial universities. Edinburgh, founded in 1583, was the most junior and the only Scottish university at that time founded after the Reformation. She enjoyed, however, a kind of preeminence over her older sisters, partly because of her internationally famous medical school and partly because of her location in the Scottish capital.

In the early summer of 1947, I noticed an advertisement announcing a position in the Department of Logic and Metaphysics. Such was the dearth of positions in the British academic world in those days, when there were hordes of eager applicants for even the least desirable vacancies, that I hardly expected more than a formal acknowledgement followed by silence. Instead, I received a brief, handwritten note from the Professor of Logic, Arthur David Ritchie, asking me to come to see him at his home on the south side of lovely George Square, which is now, alas, demolished to provide space for the new library buildings.

From the descriptions of Ritchie I had found, I somehow had expected him to be on the fierce side. I knew almost nothing about his work, much of which was in biochemistry and other scientific areas far from my own special interests. I feared the encounter with him would be intimidating.

The lean, ascetic-looking gentleman who received me spoke with quiet, gentle precision. "Fierce" was the most inapposite adjective one could have applied to him. He spoke with an occasional very slight stutter that was rather charming and seemed, as one talked with him, to be a symbol of a Quakerish reticence and a modesty that was almost absurdly self-effacing.

His first words were apologetic. He said he had read and reviewed my book (*Aesthetic Experience in Religion*, which had just been published by Macmillan) and was most interested to meet me. (I had not even seen the review, which had been favorable although mildly critical.) He told me that at the time of reviewing the book, he had somehow concluded, partly because the preface had been dated from Paris, that I was with the Foreign Office which, he added with a smile and barely noticeable stutter, had been by no means a logically warrantable conclusion. It was on account of that erroneous belief, he said, that he had been rather more critical than he might otherwise have been. Professionals are notoriously suspicious of the amateur.

His quiet graciousness put me instantly at ease. He began to talk about philosophy, inviting my opinion on its current state. As we talked for a considerable time on various philosophical topics he raised, the conversation became more and more affable.

At last he suddenly asked whether I were really interested in the position. Before I could answer he said he felt he ought to mention that there happened to be another vacancy in the Department of Moral Philosophy. Perhaps I might prefer that?¹Moral Philosophy was headed by John Macmurray, a very popular professor who attracted large classes. I replied that I had no such preference and that I should be very happy with the position for which I had applied, were I fortunate enough to be selected. Then to my astonishment he simply told me my duties and when the members of the department would meet at the beginning of term. My university teaching career was about to begin. I could not at that moment have believed that two years later my wife and I were to be sailing to America with our two small children, so that I could take up my duties as the first holder of the Rufus Jones Chair of Philosophy and Religion at Bryn Mawr.

Those two years with Ritchie were idyllic. What made them so was almost entirely the quality of his mind and the quiet radiance of his spirit. It was certainly not due to any physical comfort in the university's arrangements. Bleaker conditions for teaching would be hard to find than those prevailing at Old College, in which the department was then housed. It is called "old" not because it is anything like as old as the university, but in contrast to more recent

buildings. The architecture, from plans designed by the great Robert
Adam but much modified by William Playfair, is most handsome.

It is in a majestic, if heavy, Georgian style. The foundation stone
was laid in 1789, the year that the Bastille, fortress-like symbol of the
ancien régime and the despotism associated with it, was seized by the
Paris mob: the signal that the Revolution was underway. The college
was built, indeed, at a time when Edinburgh was attracting the
attention of the literary world and many of the younger minds at the
university were filled (some would have said infected) by the new ideas
wafted from America and France. Yet the heaviness of the building,
constructed as if to resist all the cannon of Europe, might almost
suggest that it had been intended to replace the prison fortress of Paris
by a new fortress of the Enlightenment. The building was not
completed till almost fifty years after the laying of the foundation stone
and the cupola was added much later still.

Be that as it may, there is a curiously timeless quality about the Old
Quad (as it has been for long affectionately called) that has endeared it
to the hearts of all of us who have survived the rigors of Edinburgh's
winters within its sombre walls. These walls, thick enough to exclude
even a tropical noonday sun, could be guaranteed to maintain the
entire building at a temperature at which a leg of lamb could be safely
kept in edible condition for weeks. True, there were the old steam
radiators in front of the huge, iron-barred windows; but by the time
they produced any effect the first class of the morning was over. Then,
so that there would be no danger of any warmth being wasted on an
empty classroom, the heat was turned off just as my afternoon tutorials
were beginning.

It was then that the great windows would turn to sheets of ice and a
student, clad in overcoat and sometimes even mittens and scarf, would
bring in his paper on Berkeley's immaterialism or Hume's causality and
we would sit down together, teeth chattering as our half-frozen fingers
rustled the pages. That the human brain can function at all in such a
deep freeze is a miracle of nature. That it could function well would be
too much to expect. There was an Indian restaurant close by that
served very hot curry and I sometimes went there to try to defrost at
least a small area of my torso, or else to the university Union which,
although also designed in the fortress style, was comparatively well
heated. When I went to live in the United States, people used to laugh
at me for walking through the deep snows of Pennsylvania clad only in
a tweed suit and woolen scarf. I could not have told them, for they
would not have believed, that compared with a tutorial session inside
the bleak walls of the Old Quad, a brisk walk in the snow felt quite
cosy.

So the joy of my teaching could not well be attributed to the ease of my professional surroundings. My joy in it was due mostly to Ritchie, to whom the discomfort of physical surroundings was a matter of almost complete indifference. My colleagues were interesting men, each as different from the other as chalk from cheese, different not only in temperament but in interests and concerns. They were all congenial in their various ways and I learned something from every one of them.

From David Ritchie, however, I learned more than I could repay in a lifetime. My relationship with him came at a time when I happened to be feeling somewhat jaundiced at the ways of theologians. The *odium theologicum* can be extremely oppressive, not least when to narrow prejudice are added bitterness and envy. In Ritchie I found an intellectual openness that refreshed me immeasurably and that I have never forgotten. More often than not he would step lightly into the departmental office ("retiring room" as it was called), which was a sort of backstage to the main lecture hall and where all business other than public lectures was conducted, and pop a philosophical question on an unexpected subject ranging from epistemology to ethics, from science to religion. His face would usually be bluish-red from the sharp Edinburgh wind. He was always incisive, never aggressive.

I had not been long with Ritchie before I discovered that he had never really left behind his early scientific work. Although he was dedicated to humanistic philosophy in the Socratic tradition and could turn from Aquinas to Berkeley and from Locke back to Aristotle with consummate ease, he always thought like a scientist, with a scientist's eagerness for new knowledge. It was he who showed me how close the concerns of the sciences can be to those of the religious thinker.

He disdained the logical empiricism then at the height of fashion in Oxford and Cambridge and spreading throughout the English-speaking world. In a paper published in 1937 in *Philosophy*, he attacked, in a characteristically polite but devastating way, the "Errors of Logical Positivism," showing what was wrong with its assumptions. He recognized that some of the critiques being used by the logical positivists could help to undermine various intellectual superstitions. He even went so far as to applaud them for asking certain questions "even though their answers are wrong." Their answers were wrong for more than one reason: (1) the logic was "a fallacious extension of theories applicable only to mathematics," which, unlike the empirical sciences, is a closed system, and (2) their criticisms were based on "misapprehensions as to the methods of scientific investigation," being also "mixed up with phenomenalism," a hoary philosophical error. As David Ritchie talked, you could almost see him in the physics or chemistry lab. He was especially interesting when he would casually illumine a point by relating it to scientific discoveries such as he had made about physiology and food.

He almost never alluded to organized religion as such, yet somehow one could not but detect, even apart from his Quakerish low living and high thinking, a deep, unspoken spirituality. One of Ritchie's most recurrent questions about almost all practical matters was, "Is it really necessary?" Given such an attitude as his, almost everything could seem to be not really necessary. To ask him about his religious views seemed peculiarly unnecessary.

Ritchie's views on war and pacifism are expressed in another paper, "The Ethics of Pacifism," written in 1940 and included in a delightful collection of his essays published while I was with him.[2] Characteristically, while not disguising his deep sympathies for the pacifist case, he distinguished between a true and a sham pacifism and carefully argued the merits of both sides of a seriously held pacifist position. He summed up: "The issue is between an attainable good for our country which ultimately may be no good at all, and a good not yet attainable and perhaps never to be realised on this earth. It is one aspect of the conflict between standards that are actually operative and seen in the rule of law, and ideals that are not operative but compared with which the law is hardly of value at all." In a postscript, he recognized the extreme turpitude of the Axis powers that led to World War II. Yet he affirmed that, although he might "put the emphasis differently" in view of what was then happening, both sides in the pacifist argument had a good ethical case: the pacifist one because the war then being waged had shown more than ever before "that men cannot touch pitch without being defiled" and the anti-pacifist because the same war had also made it "clearer than ever that nobody can 'contract out.' "[3]

Ritchie was so resolutely unpolitical that many did not come to know the quality of his mind and underestimated it. He lacked, too, the easy popular appeal that attracted the average student. All students taking a degree in arts had to take either his introductory course or John Macmurray's. So we got everybody, the best and the worst.

Far more students flocked to Macmurray's class. I remember Macmurray once coming to tell Ritchie that he had such a large enrollment that even his huge classroom could not accommodate them all. Would Ritchie take some of them?

Envy of his colleague's greater student popularity seemed not even to cross Ritchie's mind. Showing not a vestige either of embarrassment or of annoyance, he merely said, "Yes, of course," adding, with an elfish twinkle, "Send me all the prettiest girls!" Yet perhaps a shade of sadness lurked behind such lighthearted, jocose ripostes, for I think David knew that his razor-sharp mind carried no guarantee of appeal to mediocre ones.

Once in a while I saw him boarding or descending from a bus, but much oftener he was to be seen walking. It was, to him, the obvious way to get from one place to another. He relished wit, had a ready smile, and his eyes could flash much merriment; but only on rare occasions did he initiate talk of the trivialities that bring laughter to the lips of most of us. I suspect he did not even pause to think how Spartan a life he led. It would have seemed to him as proper to a philosopher's vocation as is celibacy to a monk's.

His wife, Katharine, brought a delightful dimension of vitality and charm to the Ritchie household. The daughter of an English prebendary, she was no doubt inured by early training to the kind of life she was to share with her husband; but her almost perpetually laughing eyes revealed a different kind of humanity from his and a lively warmth. The Ritchies were married in 1921 and had two children: a son, Justin, and a daughter, Clare. In Katharine's vivacious, ladylike way she seemed to be in a state of chronic amusement at the world in general, almost such as might be expected of a well-bred princess living among primitive tribesmen and enjoying it immensely. She was in some ways a sort of feminine version of her husband. She had an unobtrusive courage that could sometimes be awesome, as it was when I accompanied her on a hospital visit to her husband during his last illness. Knowing I could not hope ever to see him again, I kept thinking of a favorite observation of his, that we all recover from every disease but one: the one that kills us.

Katharine has kindly provided me with some surprising details about her late husband's background and early life, details one could not have guessed or, without much research, discovered. For instance, among his forebears, one was a blacksmith in the Perthshire village of Fowlis Wester and another a Presbyterian minister who had been turned out of his church for introducing a musical instrument at a time when the Scots disdained such accompaniments to the human voice in the kirk. David himself had a good ear for classical music and sometimes would even amuse himself by imitating, of all people, Harry Lauder! I should have given much to hear that performance, but alas, cordial as was our relationship, it was too professional to permit his revealing to me any such unexpected talents.

David knew the Bible well. Unlike his wife, however, he had not been brought up to regular church attendance. His father, although an instinctively religious man who read Augustine and other such literature for enjoyment and edification, had not been a churchgoer. His mother, in her widowhood, had been devout in her Anglo-Catholic way and David had been well grounded in the Anglican tradition and duly confirmed. But he seems to have regarded the Church, as did

Hegel, as a sort of religious kindergarten teaching a picturebook philosophy that was to be outgrown with intellectual maturity. Katharine reflects that her own churchgoing habits were ingrained and she never let them go, although she perceived that "he had something of a better quality of spirituality."

He did indeed. What I loved most about David Ritchie, although at the time I should never have thought of so formulating it in my mind, was his personal holiness. To some it would have seemed odd to call it that. He never mentioned the word "church" except in oblique ways and then only when a context seemed absolutely to demand it. For many years I did not even know for certain what form, if any, his Christian allegiance took. Only from the fact that on rare occasions he might quote a phrase from the Book of Common Prayer did I suppose he was an Anglican. For all I knew he might have been a vestryman in some Anglican parish, although it would have rightly seemed to me an unlikely hypothesis.

At any rate, on the one hand he never mentioned any such adherence and, on the other, he always seemed to have somewhere in his mind an oblique, quiet, cool, well-considered defense of the basic tenets of the Christian way. On occasion he would even explicitly state such a defense, but always with much verbal economy and a certain degree of reticence. He sometimes almost gave the impression of having been specially commissioned by God for a secret apostolate. Somehow it would have seemed to me outrageously bad taste to inquire into his churchmanship, if any. It would have seemed almost as brash as asking a secret service agent about the nature of his job.

He had a special interest in Berkeley and talked much about him. In one of his last letters to me, when his health was failing, he lamented that he could not get his book on Berkeley to jell. He did, however, substantially finish it and it was published posthumously.[4] Ritchie admired Berkeley, whom he believed to have been much misunderstood. As he so often said to me, Berkeley's *Theory of Vision* is the key to his thought. This last book of Ritchie's displays his characteristic incisiveness and wit and, not least, his disdain for myopic addiction to narrowminded presuppositions. He shared, in a very lively way, Berkeley's own disdain for the "minute philosophers," whether of the eighteenth or of the twentieth century, who understand neither science nor religion. Ritchie's own openness and breadth of learning and outlook were always stimulating. He was never disposed to accept the dogmas of any scholasticism, least of all the twentieth-century kind.

As Austin Farrer was pure Oxford, as Oxford indeed as Newman, whose college he for so long adorned), so Ritchie was no less Cambridge in his outlook. To his Cambridgeness he added, perhaps, another dimension, inherited from his father and his own associaton with the Scottish philosophical tradition. Still, he always seemed to me as Cambridge as the Backs. Scotland was home to him, but Cambridge had moulded his mind.

Few people could have known the full moral grandeur of Ritchie's character. His generosity towards students and others who seemed to him in genuine need and worthy of financial help that they could not obtain through the academic bureaucracy was not easily detected. He instinctively followed the Gospel injunction not to let "thy left hand know what thy right hand doeth." But not only have I accidentally discovered some of his unobtrusive acts of generosity, I have seen that, so long as the case seemed to him intrinsically deserving, it hardly occurred to him that he had any moral alternative. Such was the simplicity of his own life that he felt he could always have a little money to spare for good minds overtaken by adversity or misfortune. To have wittingly allowed his compassion to be publicly known would have seemed to him even more monstrous than not exercising it at all.

Quietness was high in his scale of values. I once mentioned to him a young colleague who was a little quiet and was a successful teacher. In another of the letters written in the years when his health was failing, he expressed his delight that quietness should succeed and cited an example out of his own experience in Manchester: another American who was silent and who also made a success of his academic career—"a quiet one," he added. He went on to contrast two exceptionally bright women students of his who in the postwar years had carried off coveted awards and won highest distinctions. One was a sophisticated, glamorous Londoner, hardworking, intelligent, and a whiz at examinations, but she never was and never could be a real philosopher. The other, lacking all such outward dazzle and shine, had turned out to be a genuine thinker. Ritchie distrusted outward brilliance as mere mental tinsel.

Once, when I was making up the list of class grades, I noticed that in a class of nearly two hundred, roughly half of whom were women, the women seemed to be noticeably better at logic but not so good at metaphysics. This was particularly striking among the top quintile of both sexes. I thought the fact worth mentioning to Ritchie, so I pointed it out to him, asking rhetorically, "Aren't women generally accounted less logical than men?" Without a moment's hesitation he replied decisively, "Bright women are very good at logic. Generally better than the men. They're not so good at metaphysics because they tend to be positivists and so don't see the point of it. But they like logic and are usually very good at it."

He probably noticed that although I was listening respectfully I did not seem entirely convinced. Then, with a mischievous chuckle he added, "It's just that they see no logical reason for applying logic to their own lives." In that bastion of male chauvinism we both smiled affably. Yet there was really very little male chauvinism in Ritchie. Whatever prejudices he had, they were not along such lines.

His unworldliness was always striking, causing him to distrust in principle all fashionable cults and their popularizers. He had a special antipathy toward Aldous Huxley, who had been in vogue among the rising postwar generation. In a letter to me, he wrote that "Aldous, clever as he is, has let the cat out of the bag. In the Rig-Veda there are hymns addressed to a deity called Soma, who may be opium, and Huxley fancies above all the deities a modern drug. But I don't suppose for a moment that it has any properties other than those of the ancient opiates and alcohol."

His distaste for Aldous Huxley was no doubt in part due to his general disparagement, which to some will seem strange in so unworldly a philosopher, of not only Hinduism but its Buddhist offshoot. He wrote me: "Of course you may say that the Buddhists have never sunk as low as this," [i.e., as low as Aldous Huxley] "but have they ever risen any higher?" He went on to admit that Buddhism may have brought about an improvement in moral conduct in the sixth century B.C., "but it is not very exciting or profitable in the twentieth A.D.—or even moral."

His prejudice against the culture and civilization of India and against those Asiatic religions that look to India as their source was indubitably rooted in an ethical judgement. He believed that they were ethically far behind all the monotheistic religions, including Islam, which had a philosophic tradition from Aristotle, fertilized by independent sources "from Persia to Spain and also Jewish, even, I suppose."

Ritchie's prejudices in such matters are of course highly questionable, to say the least, but they illustrate his profound concern for ethical conduct. Religion, in his eyes, is always peculiarly contemptible when it does not issue in a greater concern for justice and righteousness. That is, of course, precisely what is at the heart of the ethical teaching of Jesus himself.

SIX

Ian Ramsey

Ian Ramsey (1915-1972), like some of the other people described in this book, was born in humble surroundings, the son of a Lancashire postmaster and his wife. He was three before he could speak. His native ability was developed by unusual conscientiousness. That diligence, aided by the adoration of his parents and the warmth and security of his homelife, won him a scholarship to Farnworth Grammar School at the age of ten. [1]

From Farnworth, Ian won a scholarship to the University of Manchester, but declined it in favor of a place at Christ's College, Cambridge, which was also made possible by various scholarships. He lived frugally, kept exact accounts which he gave to his parents along with a present for each of them at the end of every term.

Though brought up as he was in an atmosphere of old-fashioned, north-country piety, he apparently had no thought at first of a priestly vocation. His ambitions went in a very different direction—perhaps to a career as a mathematical physicist. Then, in his first spring at Cambridge, at the age of nineteen, he developed lung trouble from a neglected cold and was forced to spend eight months in a sanitorium to recover.

It was during his stay there that he began to read more widely, including some philosophy and theology. The chaplain of his College, H.F. Woolnough, and some of the undergraduates, including some who were intending the priesthood, visited him. Ian responded eagerly to such tokens of friendship; he was a shy young man. They helped him to overcome that shyness and to talk about what was occurring in his inner spirit.

At the root of his experience was the sense of having been in danger of losing his life and of having it given back to him as a gift—a gift for a purpose. He took his recovery as a sign of God's loving care but also as his call to service. His keen mind, along with his great perseverance, won him the academic heights of a first class in both the mathematical and moral sciences tripos, followed by distinction in the theological one. Yet far more important was the extraordinary development that was gradually taking place in his spirit; certainly it did not go unnoticed by his Cambridge contemporaries.

Soon he was a Cambridge don and after some years, he was elected to a chair at Oxford in the philosophy of religion. He made a considerable intellectual impact there. At the same time, he exerted a notable pastoral influence on his students at Ripon Hall, a theological college on Boar's Hill, near Oxford. Then under the direction of one Dr. Major, the College's churchmanship was broader than most and thus controversially liberal in an old-fashioned way. There, Ian was beloved, nicknamed "panda," and elected "senior student."

In 1966, Prime Minister Harold Wilson recommended Ian for the position of Bishop of Durham, one of the greatest and most ancient of the British bishoprics. (Bishops in England are appointed by the Crown upon the recommendation of the Prime Minister, representing the party in power.) This position also made Ian a member of the House of Lords as a "spiritual peer" and he attended regularly. Politically sympathetic to the left (an inheritance from his family background), Ian made diligently prepared speeches on a wide variety of social concerns.

Taking all his duties far more seriously than do the vast majority of bishops, he overworked himself. On Easter Eve, 1972, he suffered a heart attack. Unwilling to heed the warning adequately, he died a few months later while working late over his papers in London. It was generally believed that, had he lived, he would have succeeded Arthur Michael Ramsey, Archbishop of Canterbury, a position that makes the holder the spiritual focus of the worldwide Anglican Communion.

Even in a bishop I can spy desert.
Some can be decent, even have a heart;
To some [though few] intelligence is given,
To Ramsey, every virtue under heaven.
                    —adaptation of Pope's lines in praise of Bishop Berkeley

My wife and I, in the course of one of our many return visits to the island of our birth, arrived late one Saturday evening, August 20, 1966, in our rented car, at the rather nondescript modern brick house on Harcourt Hill, near Oxford, to which our friends the Ramseys had invited us. The Ramseys, however, were anything other than nondescript. Ian, noticeably short, looked tubby enough for a mischievous fellow cleric to have called him, after the title of a church history book, "The Spread of Christianity." Such an epithet, however, could have no sting in it at all, for Ian was the most irresistibly lovable of men.

Even to me, a few years his senior, he always seemed fatherly. His whole personality breathed gentleness, compassion, and earnest human concern, all clad in a radiant bubble of merriment. The visual focus of its expression was a broad, ebullient smile. Its vocal expression came in a cheerful Lancashire speech whose matter-of-fact resonance disguised the brilliance of its owner's mind.

Nearby hovered Margaret, his blue-eyed Irish wife from Coleraine, like an angel of mercy at his side, with now and then a kindly word in her lilting Ulster speech. In the presence of their uniquely dignified simplicity of manner and style and the natural warmth of their welcome, surely no living creature could have failed to respond with affection. Certainly I have never heard of any who did not. Some might sniff or smile at Ian, according to the preconceptions they brought to him, but everybody loved him.

Yet he was by no means all mere cheeriness. Permeating his whole personality was an overriding passion for moral rectitude that is, unfortunately, by no means universal among ambassadors of Christ. If I had to sum up Ian in a single phrase, I think it would have to be: stern duty wreathed in rollicking affection for humankind. Yet it would fail to express either the keen edge of his mind or the unique warmth of his heart that seemed to be perpetually engaged in forgiving and encouraging you. He made you feel you mattered infinitely. No doubt he had imperfections like the rest of us. But never have I met a man more completely human in the Socratic sense or more thoroughly humane.

At the time of that visit he was fifty-one, the Nolloth Professor of the Philosophy of the Christian Religion and Fellow of Oriel. Our acquaintance went back to the late forties, when he had written me from Christ's College, Cambridge, asking me to come there to meet his students and discuss with them the book I had just published. Unfortunately, his letter had come at a particularly busy time and I had felt unable to accept. So I sent him a polite letter of regret. Had I but known then what a wonderful person he was, I would no doubt have made a Herculean effort. But alas, I did not know, and it was to be many years before we actually met.

He kept in touch with me, however, and at last, in 1963, when he wrote to tell me that he was lecturing at various American institutions on the Atlantic seaboard, I was able to have him invited to give a summer course at the University of Southern California. The Ramseys instantly became our friends. Later, they stayed at our home for a month with their younger son, Vivian, while I happened to be on a similar assignment at the University of British Columbia. In 1965 we stayed with them at Oxford for a few days and did so again the following year, when we were once again briefly in England.

No sooner had I sat down with him that Saturday night in 1966 than he beamed even more boyishly than usual, his eyes twinkling with merriment, a rich north-country vitality in his quietly excited voice. "We're leaving Oxford," he announced. My face expressed surprise, not to say dismay, for he was at the height of his influence there as an intellectual champion of Christian faith in a hostile environment.

Seeing the disappointment on my face, he said teasingly, "I'll give you three guesses where we're going!"

For my part, a little tired after a long drive on what had then become for me the "wrong" side of the road, I must have looked a little despairing, for he characteristically came to my rescue with a sporting encouragement, "I'll give you a clue. It's not academic. It's ecclesiastical."

Any meagre knowledge I might ever have had of Church of England politics had by then almost totally vanished, so I had to struggle manfully with shots in the ecclesiastical dark.

"Dean of Winchester?" I suggested intrepidly.

"No."

"Dean of York?"

"No, but you're getting hot. Right part of the country."

"Dean of Durham?"

"*Bishop* of Durham," he corrected, as though striking a *t* in a boy's exercise and giving him a courtesy pass.

Matching his mischievous mood I protested that the game had been unfair from the start. "How was I to know?" I complained with mock indignation. "If only you had told me of the change of policy—this recommending of intelligent people for the episcopate—I could have got it right the first time."

When the laughter had subsided he went on to describe some of the circumstances attending his appointment. He told me that when he had received the formal letter from the Prime Minister, asking in the customary way for Ramsey's consent to the proposed recommendation to the Queen, the envelope looked so like a piece of junk mail that he had it almost in the trash basket before he decided to glance at its contents. Some might wonder whether, in later years amidst the exasperations that would attend him in his See, he might have wished he had never retrieved that letter.

Ian was a model bishop, for he was an able and a truly good man. He threw himself into his work with the same conscientiousness that he had approached every duty from childhood onwards. Indeed, within six years he literally worked himself to death trying, at an unusually difficult time, to fulfill his episcopal duties in terms of his conception of his functions.

No one could have called him too good for this world. He was too deeply in love with all around him for that to be said. Some, no doubt, thought him too good for the House of Lords, of which, by ancient prerogative, his position as bishop automatically made him a member. He spoke there with vigor and candor, in season and out, whenever he felt the duty to do so—which was very often indeed and sometimes to the considerable discomfiture of his august audience.

Ian's churchmanship was never obtrusive, but no one with any sense of Catholic tradition could fail to perceive its riches were largely hid from him. Of course he knew the early Fathers and had a working acquaintance with medieval thought. But on the whole his mind moved in other directions.

Some say that Ian, toward the end of his life, showed a Catholic influence in his churchmanship, alien though it was to his training and nurture. It may be so; but if it were, it cannot be attributed to any influence at Headington Quarry when Ian was a curate there. For while it is true that that parish had been under Tractarian influence since 1867, a vicar presented to the living in 1935 changed that tradition, abolishing the Sung Mass and other such usages. That "low church" period endured from 1935 till 1947, prevailing there at the time of Ian's curacy.

Canon Head, the present vicar of the parish, tells me that Ian, while he was there, presented it with a copy of the 1928 Prayer Book; but no special significance can be attributed to that. Ian was far too openminded to harbor vulgar prejudices against "high church" ways or against anything else in the variegated pattern of man's worship of God. But in my experience he never seemed to feel at home in an atmosphere of Catholic churchmanship. Many will regret this, not least since historically so much of the social concern that has shown itself within the Church of England and that was so dear to Ian's own heart has been cradled in that particular tradition.

Apart from his passionate interest in social conditions that sprang from his love of people and was so well informed by his own early life, Ian's consuming interest lay in trying to build a bridge between analytical philosophy and philosophical theology. In the intellectual climate of Oxford at that time, almost nothing could have been a more unpopular undertaking; but although Ian was exceptionally sensitive to the feelings of others, he did not care a button what people thought when he believed the truth was at stake. If a mission involved no challenge, how could it be worth undertaking?

His concern for the marriage of philosophy and religion was expressed in his lectures and his daily discussions with students in his bookstuffed rooms in Oriel and in the succinct style of his writings.[2] It was in his work in this area that I knew Ian Ramsey best. His approach and his vocabulary differed somewhat from my own but I deeply sympathized with his thrust, appreciated his mathematical mind, and learned in a new way how in the nature of things those who have none of Ramsey's openness to persons and sensitivity to the universe cannot "see" God.

Perhaps in his effort to communicate in the idiom of his day, he adhered too narrowly both to the fashionable logic and to the biblical way of expressing the nature of God. Perhaps he took too seriously both the philosophical and the theological fashions of his day. If so, it was because he so readily responded to whatever was confronting him in persons or in things.

But in this area of thought his greatest handicap was probably his own goodness—he honestly expected others to be as sensitive morally as he was himself. As he saw the best in other people, so he saw also the good in the universe and discerned in it a purpose that not everyone is equipped to perceive. For, after all, what we see outside us mirrors what we are ourselves. Ian was pervaded by a dimension of being that transcends what most men and women find either in what we call nature or even in what we call "other persons." His weakness, if it can be called a weakness, was that he could not accept the fact that trained minds can be more blindly insensitive to the "voice of the angels" than some comparatively untrained minds such as his own parents'. There are some things a loving heart will never understand, not least when, as in Ian's case, it is conjoined with a razorsharp mind.

Yet there was little he did not know about injustice and moral degradation. He had seen them in the depression and unemployment of the drab factories and mines around Bolton, the Lancashire area where he had lived as a boy. His expression of moral indignation could sometimes make him look slightly funny. I recall his recounting how, while driving across the United States, he was arrested in a remote area for speeding. He had run into a speed trap devised, no doubt, chiefly to supply local or state funds. From what we know of Ian's habits he probably had carefully calculated his speed down to a decimal point below the limit.

Finding the arresting officer indifferent to his arguments, he demanded to see the local judge. The latter was eventually traced, sitting in a rocking chair on the patio of his rural home. Ian insisted that in no circumstances would he plead guilty as the judge suggested would be advisable, for he was in fact innocent. The judge, unaccustomed to such concern for moral rectitude, explained that if he wished to plead not guilty he would have to attend court, which would delay his journey for many days. The accused Ian said he was perfectly willing to contribute the seventeen dollars that was described as a fine, so long as he did not have to plead guilty to a transgression he had not committed.

In the end the judge agreed that this could be done. How it was contrived I do not know, but I suspect the judge promised the accused a clean slate and then afterwards simply wrote up the incident as a normal plea of guilty to justify the fine. At any rate, Ian's description of the event that most people would have merely written off as a piece of bad luck sounded a little funny to us who knew him. No doubt the perplexed judge would have taken him to be an unusually eccentric foreigner. Ian's moral fastidiousness might even have seemed to him a mild form of insanity.

Wherever we went together in Los Angeles he always behaved naturally, speaking to waitresses with the same respect for human dignity he would have accorded a duchess. Even the most tiresome people grew somehow more lovable when they basked in the sunshine of his interest and the green pastures of his concern. When I revisited a little restaurant in the Mexican quarter to which I had taken him a week earlier, a young waitress asked, "Who is your friend? He is so good, so good." Then she cried softly, murmuring in half-Spanish, "I wish he was my father." She was not alone. No one could ever remain completely orphaned who had ever crossed Ian's path.

When Ian talked of others he almost always had something good to say even about the dimmest of them. It was as if he had a mental index card with the bad things all in invisible ink and always at least something positive about them in bold print. He absolutely never gossiped. Only once, when I mentioned a man who was under consideration for a visiting position in California and who, I later discovered, would have been morally and mentally a disaster, did Ian's charitableness break down. Yet after a lengthy pause he said only, in an impressively subdued tone, "Geddes, I would just offer a word of caution there." Ian could be very eloquent in a few words of that kind.

Among his many intellectual interests was the work of that eighteenth-century thinker, George Berkeley, himself an Irish bishop. In an article, "Berkeley and the Possibility of an Empirical Metaphysics," published in 1966, he said very characteristically, "Creedal affirmations can only be made adequately in the context of

Christian behavior."[3] No doubt there was an affinity between Ian and Berkeley in outlook even more than in thought.

As a class, bishops are not widely admired. One need not be a Puritan to echo Milton's indictment:

Blind mouths! that scarce themselves know how to hold
A sheep-hook or have learned aught else the least
That to the faithful herdman's art belongs.[4]

Of course there are exceptions, and how easily could one adapt and paraphrase the lines of Pope, substituting such names as one's charity dictated and Ian's, of course for Berkeley's:

Even in a bishop I can spy desert;
Secker is decent, *Rundel* has a heart:
Manners with candour are to *Benson* given,
To *Berkeley*, every virtue under heaven.[5]

What less can one say of a man so honest as to record in *Who's Who* as his principal recreations "family and home."? Then after a semicolon came his subordinate ones, which he designated "reading maps and (once) Bradshaw."[6] Ian's boyish sense of humor never left him, even under the weight of the burdens that he took too seriously for the good of his own health.

The grandeur of Durham Cathedral, not least as seen from the river Wear below, and the magnificence of Auckland Castle, made little impression on Ian except as reminders of the immensity of his duties. Durham is one of the three most important Sees in England, after Canterbury and York. In the Middle Ages, the bishops of Durham held immense civil as well as ecclesiastical jurisdiction, ranking as Counts Palatine, and the See has since been occupied by many distinguished churchmen. It is virtually impossible to take a photograph of Auckland Castle, other than an aerial one, that would give any adequate idea of its immensity.[7]

According to a fairly plausible journalistic story, when reporters asked Ramsey what was the first act he would do on entering upon his new duties at Durham, he replied, "Oonpahk." I hardly think the Lancashire accent could have been quite as broad as reporters loved to make it, but the practicality was pure Ramsey. Ian was always extremely practical. Moreover, he saw nothing in the least unpractical about theology or metaphysics. He did sometimes like to project a "working class" image. I understand he arrived at Buckingham Palace, for instance, wearing a cloth cap.

Ian was resolved, when he went to Auckland Castle, to involve himself in every facet of the life of the people. At home by temperament and upbringing with the north-country style and outlook, he was not long in understanding the technical details of the various key industries in his diocese. By the time of our first visit he seemed a master of the situation.

His pastoral concern for clergy in trouble or distress was well known. Yet despite all the astounding skill and devotion he brought to his very difficult task, some of the less educated clergy grumbled that he was too intellectual, that he had never been a parish priest. Such ignorant prejudice always pained Ian because he knew so well how vulnerable is the Church to criticism as a bastion of nonthink. True, he did speak on a high level, thereby winning many supporters among thoughtful people in all walks of life. But not only was he criticized by those who could never hope to come anywhere near following his thought or appreciating its gigantic scope; he was a natural target for the partisans of vested interests who felt threatened by his sometimes daring, not to say revolutionary, proposals for social reform.

He pled strongly for prison reform, insisting that prison must be both punishment and the possibility of rehabilitation. He urged conjugal visits for prisoners. He attacked *apartheid*. He carried such questions and much, much more into the House of Lords, where many felt that he spoke too much and too often.

He worked incessantly. Every moment was utilized. He was chauffeured from Auckland Castle to the London train, writing a speech he was to deliver in the Lords. Often he would speak there extempore on subjects that many felt to be beyond the concern of a bishop. To Ian, however, there was no such subject, since the spiritual and the material were in his eyes inextricably woven together. Wherever human beings were in relation to one another in any way whatsoever, moral issues arose. He simply could not say no. Even in the midst of his extremely busy life he found time, while I was a guest at Auckland Castle on three occasions, to talk, if only in a few minutes snatched between pressing duties, as we had talked in the past of the great moral and theological issues that were never really out of his mind. The Castle also served as a diocesan conference center. It was a busy place as well as a peaceful haven.

Perhaps it is because he was always so much more than anything he could say or do, gifted though he was, that in my memory of his presence, trivial incidents keep bobbing up in my mind. During one of my visits to the Castle, for instance, Margaret suggested a trip to a local market, saying that Ian would be too busy to join us. But he suddenly appeared with that curious, almost laughable and very characteristic raising of the eyebrows in a look of expectancy. Join us he did. And in that market, old men and women, young lads and lasses, greeted him as spontaneously as they would have greeted a friend in a neighboring cottage, yet with an affection and respect that they would have bestowed on hardly anyone else. In his presence they always looked as though they were breathing in fresh air. Nor did any such obvious admiration ever seem to affect his easy friendliness. Ian was fundamentally unspoilable. Much of his charm lay in his never having quite grown up. He was a kind of ecclesiastical Peter Pan with a prodigious mind.

He was very widely recognized as a political liberal, even radical. Many in the Establishment thought he used his position as the bishop of an historic See to propagate political ideologies that are be no means to be identified with the Christian Way. The charge has much truth in it. Certainly he never sought to please or even to be conciliatory towards the Establishment. If only he had addressed himself to social injustice out of his own background and experience, he might have been more persuasive and his voice on these matters more authentic, more like that of the biblical prophets. Alas, his kind of political leftism seemed to owe more to the leftwing intellectuals who had overshadowed his experience with doctrinaire theory.

I think that was a pity, for it may have somewhat obstructed his ability to speak for the people for whom he wanted to speak. The "drawingroom socialism" of Oxford and Cambridge could obscure the authentic Christian message he was so well qualified to convey, diminishing both his effectiveness in voicing social wrongs and his persuasiveness in conveying them to his hearers. His heart was right; certainly he knew better. But years of listening to the nostrums of clever, well-to-do young people bent on straightening out society from text books in economics and political science may have injured his native authenticity in the expression of moral concern. Happily, he was always better than anything he could ever say.

What a bishop! One wonders whether, if he had lived longer, he could really have done much more. In knowledgeable circles in England, many thought of him as the inevitable successor for the primatial See of Canterbury when it would become vacant. Certainly there seemed to be nobody in all England who could have been deemed in any important respect more eminently well qualified. But they, like Ian himself, probably underestimated the forces of conservatism in Church and State. English conservatism operates in peculiarly subtle ways. To many Ian looked somewhat like a reincarnation of William Temple, also both a philosopher in his day and a resolute campaigner in the field of social action. In fact, however, he was in many ways notably unlike Temple.

Indeed, Ian was unlike anybody else. His kind of goodness was unique, as were the shape of his personality and the cast of his mind.

Above all, when you companied with him alone, you somehow knew you were in the presence of a unique kind of spiritual and mental health. His books were carefully written, the best of his lectures strikingly well organized; but Ian was more, far more, than the best of his lectures and the finest of his writings.

His inability to say no to opportunities to communicate with business executives, factory workers, Sunday school teachers, farmers, or peers of the realm, commissions of Church or State, precipitated his death. On Easter Eve, 1972, he suffered a severe heart attack. The doctors urged him to go easy. For a few months he did, for he was by nature a sensible man and obedient to reasonable authority. He spent several months at Auckland Castle and in the Lake District, convalescing and enjoying leisure with Margaret. Yet it was also not in his nature to go on like that for very long. To him, it would have seemed like preferring rust to wear.

Invitations came along; opportunites arose. He found it difficult to say no even to jobs not really worth his time. In July, he was asked to be chairman of the Central Religious Advisory Committee of the BBC. He accepted. On October 6, after chairing one of its meetings in London, he stayed on in the council chamber intending to do some other work before going home.

After some minutes a janitor came into the room to clear up. He greeted the bishop, who made to reply but after a word or two fell forward on the table at which he was writing. Medical help was swift, but within fifteen minutes he was dead. It was a dramatic, yet in some ways a curiously fitting way for death to come to him. He had, with such prodigality, spent his life in his work, as though he dared not waste a moment of the precious time he believed had been given him for the purpose he had discerned as a shy Cambridge undergraduate recuperating in an English sanitorium.

Ian Ramsey

James J. Cleland

René Le Senne

SEVEN

James Cleland

James Cleland (1903-1978) was the son of a Presbyterian minister,
a former carpenter who had founded the Lodging House Mission in a
Glasgow slum. His father died when Jim was only twelve and this
played a part in Jim's resolve to enter the ministry.

Graduated from the University of Glasgow in 1924, with his
theological degree from there in 1927, he studied for an additional
year at Union Theological Seminary in New York, where he came
under the influence of its president, Henry Sloane Coffin.

Although he was unmistakably a preacher before all else, he had
considerable ability as a New Testament scholar and began his
teaching career, on Coffin's recommendation, as an instructor at
Amherst College in 1931. He remained there until 1945, when he
accepted the James B. Duke Chair of Preaching at Duke University,
becoming also the first person at that institution to hold the title of
Dean of Chapel. He remained at Duke for the balance of his life.

He lectured widely at American institutions and often, on summer
visits to Scotland, preached from prominent pulpits. A member of Phi
Beta Kappa, he received honorary doctorates from his alma mater as
well as from American universities. Ill health plagued him in his later
years; yet he remained not only active but ever ready to make light of
his own misfortunes and to help others in theirs.

Blessed are the debonair.

No one who thinks all Scots dour could have known Jim Cleland,
for whom no adjective could have been more inapposite. While he was
a Scottish Presbyterian *pur sang,* he was also a one-of-a-kind expatriate

Scot. Indeed he was altogether one of a kind. In 1954 he wrote, "Maybe there is room for a new beatitude: 'Blessed are the debonair,' in whom the Word of God sparkles with graciousness and charm."

Jim was always debonair, whether in the pulpit, where he was a peerless master of the preacher's craft, or socially where his gifts as a raconteur delighted thousands. He had a lightness of touch that captured even the most sullen and an understanding and compassion for people that won even the hardest of hearts. As his hobby he listed "collecting people and stories." The collector, however, was probably more remarkable than anything or anyone in his collection. Perhaps by *de-bon-air* Jim included the fresh breezes of his native heath; at any rate the atmosphere he created wherever he went was no less uniquely refreshing.

The worst thing I know that could be said of Jim is that he was a workaholic. He knew it and freely admitted it. He would spend as much as fifteen hours preparing a sermon. His sermons were always carefully typed and almost never exceeded twenty minutes to deliver. Yet they sounded spontaneous and (alas, how rare among preachers!) his hearers often wished he had not stopped so soon. Although he came to the pulpit in full clerical dress and with a dignified presence, he never left behind him the puckish wit that endeared him to everyone wherever he went. Yet even while he was keeping people roaring with laughter he always seemed to be *on duty*, whether he was in the pulpit on a stately occasion or squatting on the floor munching peanuts at a family get-together.

His mother was doubtful about her son's ability to follow in his father's footsteps. Even late in life, her doubts continued. When he was invited to preach at Wellington Church, Glasgow, she counseled him to accept but not to go, since she did not think he was good enough for such an important pulpit. Jim often said that his mother never could understand how Jesus could have been a Jew since he was a Presbyterian. So perhaps she never did quite understand either her son's gifts or the scale of the land of his adoption.

For all the misgivings Jim's mother expressed about his abilities, there can be little doubt that inwardly she cherished the highest hopes for him, concentrating far more attention on him than on his sister or brother. While she noted his academic successes as they came along, she feared they might go to his head. Jim's widow, Alice, tells me that his mother urged her to keep him humble.

Alice recounts that, when the University of Glasgow made him an honorary doctor of divinity, "it was Mother Cleland Day, the fulfillment of all" her dreams. (Jim once told me that although he had already received an honorary degree from an American institution, his mother did not think that anything other than a Scottish one really counted!) When she heard him preach, she said, "You're a better preacher than ever I thought you would be, but you are not as *good* a man as your father." By this time, however, he was in his early fifties and his mother was forced to admit that he was now grown up.

Alice and Jim met while he was at Union in 1927-28 and she at Teacher's College, Columbia University. They were introduced through Scottish friends at International House where she was staying. He was one of a group that had been scheduled to exhibit Scottish folk dancing at the house and, when his partner had fallen ill, he asked Alice if she would substitute. Though of Scottish ancestry, she demurred on the ground that she was an American and the Scots might on that account resent having their dances exhibited by her. Jim rejoined, "You'll do all right if you keep your mouth shut!"[1] They were married in 1932.

Jim was always understood. His lilting speech carried echoes of his Glasgow boyhood but it was eminently intelligible to all. People thought he had a "Scotch brogue" but that was because they had never heard real Glasgow, which Professor Higgins might have called "Scotch Cockney" and not without reason, since it is about as unintelligible as London's rhyming slang.[2]

Nor was Jim ever at a loss to know how to turn social embarrassment into laughter. At a formal dinner the toastmaster forgot to invite him to say grace till dinner was well under way. Asked if it were too late, Jim jumped to his feet, tapped his glass to request silence and said, "Bless the Lord, O my soul, and all that is *within* me, praise his holy name."

During my own decade at Bryn Mawr he came to preach unfailingly at the College every year, captivating the girls with his witty style and winsome delivery. Bryn Mawr (in those days, at any rate) was a conspicuously "secular" place, but on a Cleland weekend it seemed almost as if church bells were ringing. He usually stayed through Monday to answer students' questions and talk over their problems.

Jim's habitual use of the clerical collar may have owed something to his early training at Dunblane Cathedral where, before coming to his first position in the United States, he had had a stint as assistant under Dr. Hutchison Cockburn, a Scottish Presbyterian ecclesiastic of enormous stature and formidable presence, who later became one of the presidents of the controversial World Council of Churches at Geneva. Cockburn, having found his assistant cycling around the parish in "plus-fours" and a cap, rebuked him with the words, "Young man, in future you will wear your "dog" collar always; it's the most spiritual thing about you."

Jim's claim that his hobby was "collecting people and stories" was really an act of self-defense; he had no hobbies. When people talked to him of their collections he would say, "I'd like to show you my collection of teabag labels." (He did in fact keep old teabag labels in an empty receptacle and when it was full he tossed them away and started all over again.) When he saw the look of boredom descend upon and overshadow his friends' faces he would go on, "Well, maybe I should wait till I have mounted them properly." He was rewarded with a look of gratitude.

"I wear old clothes and buy new books and smoke the kind of pipe tobacco my friends give me," he was heard to say. He was seldom seen outside church without a pipe in his hand. Alice insists, however, that he "smoked matches" rather than tobacco. An avid reader, he used his personal inclination to serve the best needs of his work. He could summarize the latest novel everybody had read (or pretended to have read) and go on to make a strikingly telling sermon point out of it without sounding like a preacher at all. He also found time to write. His four books, all homiletic and pastoral, include *The True and Lively Word* and *Preaching to Be Understood*.

He was one of the few persons outside the medical profession to have been elected to Alpha Omega Alpha, the honor medical society. His own colleagues loved him. Businessmen and people in all walks of life and from all over the United States were drawn to Jim like nails to a magnet, because he seemed to understand their needs and fears and aspirations even before they spoke of them. The students in one of the dormitories called it affectionately "Cleland House."

Perhaps what most of all endeared him to his hearers was that quality of being always *on duty as a man of God* and loving every minute of his work. In that, of course, he was not entirely unique. However, he combined with that quality another in which lay indeed much of Jim's secret—he always did his homework.

He was both so talented and so industrious that what came across from him at all times, even before one felt his loving concern, could be summed up in one word—competence. Remarkably few preachers have this quality. It is a quality which, when baldly stated, sounds almost pedestrian, perhaps even a damning-with-faint-praise; but it made Jim's personality solid gold, inspiring a unique kind of confidence as soon as he appeared on the scene. It was by reason of this quality of competence, too, that Jim could get away with witty fireworks and sparks of levity even on grave and solemn occasions. You always knew what Jim was about, because he so obviously knew it himself. Then as his heart opened up, as it did as soon as he began anything, the hearts of his hearers melted like snow on a sunny day.

A good actor makes fiction sound like truth; most preachers can make truth sound like fiction. Jim, however, was happily free of anything remotely like the notorious "parson's voice." In his prayers as in his sermons, at weddings as at funerals, he spoke in a loud voice but in a strikingly conversational tone, somewhat high pitched, like that of a happy child pleading with his parents. He made even the most conventional and traditional phrases sound as if he had just coined them for the first time in human history. He was a consummate craftsman in the art of preaching, yet he gave the impression of having no craftsmanship at all, knowing as he did that the greatest art is to conceal art.

In the kind of public worship in which he was engaged, conventional styles can be excruciating and he knew it. A studied and exaggerated informality can be even more exasperating, and he knew that too. Instead, he radiated a naturalness that sprang largely from the fact that he was never in any way self-conscious about his faith. It was as much a part of his personality as is the alphabet part of a writer's stock-in-trade and numbers part of a mathematician's mind.

He wore his clerical collar as a proud soldier his uniform. He was both a Scottish Presbyterian thoroughbred and, by adoption, a good American. He was nothing if not a pilgrim, having, as the writer to the Hebrews puts it, "no continuing city"; yet he was passionately devoted to every place he lived in. By "place," however, Jim always meant "people," for to him that was the real world. The rest was mere wrapping. That was one reason why he could so easily evoke both their love and their respect.

Yet he could evince a streak of acerbity, too, in his own kindly way, when things did not go as he thought they should. Although he never stood on dignity, he liked respect. I remember once entering Taylor Hall at Bryn Mawr to lead him to a class he was to address, when an avalanche of girls came pouring down the stairs like a horde of Valkyries rushing headlong to report to Odin their latest catch for Valhalla. We barely withstood the stampede. When it was over he looked at me inquiringly. I asked what was troubling him. "They look as though they wouldn't stand aside even for a pregnant cripple," he murmured disconsolately. But in a moment he was his cheerful self again.

On one of the innumerable occasions when he accepted a preaching engagement, his hosts in some remote place in the American heartland gave him an honorarium of five dollars, which even in those days would hardly have bought him a good meal. When an apology was proffered with the check, Jim waved the apology aside with the observation that he was always satisfied with whatever people felt they could afford the laborer they had hired. "Just one thing, though," he then added. "If you give five dollars to a professor of preaching, what's your rate for a theological student?" No doubt faces reddened a bit, but Jim would say it in such a kindly way that people would not harbor resentment even if the guilt they felt lay on them like a suet dumpling in their stomachs. There was never any rancor in even his sternest rebuke. What he rebuked was always in one way or another lack of love. For Jim that was the only sin worth talking about.

He had a very deep affection for and understanding of his Scottish homeland, to which in summer he was a frequent visitor. He received many invitations to preach in Scottish pulpits such as St. George's West, Edinburgh, and he rarely could resist an opportunity to do so. To him such invitations came neither as a duty nor as an honor; they just seemed natural things for him to accept. A soldier does not demur when called to the battlefield, even when his mother doubts his worthiness to go!

The armed forces, too, used him and sent him to many countries. "The difference between preaching to servicemen and preaching to students," Jim observed, "is not as great as you might think. The message is the same, only the illustrations are different. Some people ask me how I can preach at the Pentagon. I go into the Pentagon the same way as I go into the Duke Chapel—as a sinner speaking to other sinners." After spending one Christmas in Greenland he quipped, "Well, Cardinal Spellman couldn't go and Bob Hope couldn't go, so I went."

When he arrived at Duke, soccer was not an official sport; it was only a club sport. The Duke football coach, Wallace Wade, urged Jim to coach soccer, a task he duly undertook as part of the work of the Lord on top of his heavy load of teaching and preaching.

Once he was invited to a university in Texas as a special preacher and, upon his return to Duke, was ready to write a note of thanks to the Chancellor for having invited him. He found, however, that the latter had forestalled him with a letter of profuse thanks telling him he had made hundreds of new friends because he did everything so well. This evoked from Jim a letter that began, "Like God, you 'prevented' me." Then, taking up a remark by the Chancellor about his accomplishments, he went on, "Perhaps what does encourage some humility in me is that I do not really like to preach. Now I do have pride about refereeing a soccer game. I was a good referee!" Perhaps he was. I had no opportunity to judge his talents in that capacity. I can only say that he looked as unlike a soccer referee as anyone I have ever known. Yet I am sure that when he took on a referee's job he would do it, as he did everything else, with singular dedication. Once again his secret was native ability combined with the unremitting toil that he thoroughly enjoyed.

Knowing the value of hard work in the conduct of the holy ministry, he cautioned divinity students never to rely on mere slick, off-the-cuff remarks in the pulpit or elsewhere. To illustrate his point he told of a young minister who tried to comfort a bereaved family and who, pointing to the corpse, declared, "Friends, what you see here is only the bare shell. The nut is gone."

How well he knew that the greatest art is to conceal art! When he went to a prep school to speak, everyone thought him very witty and spontaneous to come up with the grace he offered as the hungry boys stood, mouths watering for the breakfast that was on the table, "Praise God for eggs and buttered toast; Father, Son and Holy Ghost." But Jim had probably pondered carefully the evening before what would be the best grace for the occasion. He had a great sense of the fitting and to his way of thinking, the kindly was always fitting.

His lectures, mainly on preaching, which he delivered in many universities and other institutions, inevitably were filled with his delightful stories, devices he used to convey to his hearers the wisdom he had to impart and wanted them to assimilate. Jim had a remarkable knack of letting you see yourself in all your weakness and folly without causing you to feel in any way resentful, however alarming the picture might be.

When he addressed the annual banquet of the St. Andrew's Society of the State of New York in 1950, he spoke of a Scottish minister who told his flock that there is no such being as the Devil. One of his elders asked him afterwards if he really meant that the Devil does not exist. He nodded. The elder looked quite crestfallen as he murmured, "Oh dear, I feel as though I had lost a personal friend."

On the same occasion Jim told his audience that he was a very bad sailor and suffered from seasickness as soon as there was the slightest roll. Crossing the Atlantic once on the *Caledonia* (one of the old Anchor Line vessels), he was on the verge of being sick when the captain (Captain Collie) asked him to preach. "I'm going to be sick," he told Collie, who replied that preaching is a fine cure for seasickness. Jim protested that he could be spectacularly sick right in the middle of a sermon. At last the captain said, "Padre, you've *got* to preach. For the last three voyages we've had nothing but damned Episcopal services." To this Jim replied that perhaps in such an emergency the Lord would uphold him. He preached and the Lord upheld.

Alice told me that, as anyone who knew Jim might well have expected, he kept a file of his stories carefully organized for use on specific occasions with captions such as "Medical," "Scottish," and even "Immortality, Intimations of." Some were merely devices for capturing attention; others had more profound significance. One that he claimed to be true was of a Scotswoman who was being married for the seventh time in the same church by the same minister who remarked jocosely before the service that he really could not promise to go on and on like this. She silenced him with, "Meenister, if the Lord keeps on takin' them, who am I to say I'll no dae the same?"

Jim liked stories with a macabre twist to them, such as one about a man whose wife was in her coffin and being carried downstairs when one of the bearers slipped at a corner and banged the coffin against a wall, whereupon the lid fell off and the corpse sat up. That was that, and she was duly taken back upstairs. In a few months, however, she really did die and was carried down the same stairs. As the bearers reached the point of the first misadventure the husband cried out, "Watch that corner, boys." A variant of this story of Jim's appeared in *The Reader's Digest* fourteen years after his death.

Under the caption "Love Your Enemies" is the story of the little boy whose Sunday School teacher told him the sad story of the early Christians' being thrown to the lions, which she illustrated with slides. When the boy looked sad, she tried to comfort him with the assurance that the Christians would all be going to heaven. That was not what was troubling him. He had noticed a wee lion in the corner who didn't have a Christian.

He knew, too, how to titillate his audience without offending the sensibilities of the straight-laced. A favorite gambit for a sermon on marital jealousy was the story of Adam's coming home late one night and of Eve's accusing him of having an affair with another woman. Adam reminded her that there *were* no other women; she was literally the only girl in the world. Nevertheless, that night, when Adam was asleep, she counted his ribs.

Jim had a special repertoire of such stories, designed to exhibit the absurdity, not to say the irreligiosity, of biblical literalism. A boy, asked what he had learned at Sunday School, reported to his mother that his teacher had told them that God had sent Moses behind the enemy lines to rescue the Israelites from the Egyptians. When they came to the Red Sea, Moses called the engineers to build a pontoon bridge. When they had all crossed the bridge they looked back and saw the Egyptian tanks coming, whereupon Moses called his HQ by radio to send bombers to blow up the bridge. "Bobby!" his mother exclaimed. "Is that really how the teacher told the story?" "No," admitted Bobby. "But if I told it her way you'd never believe it."

Yet he was at his best in bringing comfort in time of sorrow or distress. Visiting a sick friend in a hospital one day, he heard of a man who had been paralyzed from the neck down and was facing being a quadraplegic for the rest of his life. He went over at once to see him.

Discovering that, by coincidence, the patient was a fellow Glaswegian, he started singing an old Scottish folk song. Soon the man was joining in and eventually the whole ward was singing the twenty-third psalm to the tune *Orlington*. The radiance on the man's face showed that there had been no need for a formal benediction. Jim Cleland could bring the Viaticum on a mere song or funny story.

Unexpectedly, perhaps, in a man famed above all as a preacher, Jim was happier in the classroom than in the pulpit. He preached as a matter of duty, developing his skill as a raconteur as part of the preacher's craft and in obedience to Paul's injunction to become a fool for Christ's sake. Moreover, although he talked much about his native Scotland and spoke at St. Andrew's Society banquets and the like, he had less pride in ancestry than some might have supposed. Nor had he any real interest in material things. All he wanted were books and a large desk. He was indeed a pilgrim, but one who left deep footprints behind him; footprints that now seem very vestiges of the One he tried so faithfully to serve.

Although his very florid face, shining eyes, and laughing lips made him look, at least in his younger days, the picture of health, Jim unfortunately suffered much from kidney and other troubles and endured a great deal of pain through much of his working life. Sometimes he had a haggard look as if racked with pain. Yet even then he always managed a smile and a word of cheer.

When Jim retired in 1968, letters poured in from his vast army of admirers and friends. When he died ten years later, tributes came from every quarter. Humble folk joined with the great in celebrating the memory of his goodness. A joint resolution was passed by the Senate and the House of Representatives of the State of North Carolina honoring his memory and praising his work. Many spoke of his gifts: his warmth, his generosity of spirit, his compassion, his tolerance, his indefatigable zeal, his light touch, his persuasiveness, and his infectious laughter. To me, however, the most discerning of all the remarks made in this avalanche of eulogizing was one that alluded to the personal holiness of the man.

For that was above all what Jim was: a holy man. Even as he laughed and clowned in his inimitably natural way, he was exuding a personal holiness that constantly transfigured him. Surely, he was one of the best preachers I have ever known. Yet he preached even better still when he was not preaching at all, when he was just chatting with you by the fireside or in a railroad train where as likely as not he would be regaling you with his latest story, his laughing eyes penetrating yours with a glow of holy love.

Humor is, of course, anarchistic and irreverent by its very nature.

EIGHT

René Le Senne

René Le Senne (1882-1954) was educated in his native France, attending the Ecole Normale Supérieure, taking his *agrégation* in philosophy (the standard competitive examination through which one gains entry into teaching positions), and eventually obtaining the higher French doctorate (*docteur-ès-lettres*) that is the gateway to university positions. After teaching at various lycées, notably the Lycée Louis-le-Grand in Paris, he returned to a teaching appointment at the Ecole Normale Supérieure, then went on to university positions, eventually being appointed to the chair of *morale* (moral philosophy or ethics) at the Sorbonne. He held this position till his retirement in 1952, when he was accorded the status of honorary professor. A foreign member of many learned societies in Italy, Germany and Spain (including the Accademia dei Lincei), he received an honorary doctorate from the University of Louvain and, in the following year (1948), was elected a member of the Institut de France, which consists of the French Academy and four other academies of a more specialist character—in his case the Academy of Moral and Political Science. He was also an *officier de la Légion d'Honneur*.

The author of many books and articles on philosophy, he collaborated with Louis Lavelle in editing a collection consisting of more than sixty philosophical books. This collection (*Collection Philosophie de l'Esprit*) was specifically founded to defend metaphysical enterprise in philosophy against its positivistic critics at a time when logical empiricism was challenging traditional philosophical undertakings all over Europe, becoming the dominating force in academic philosophy throughout the English-speaking world. Nihilistic forms of existentialism were beginning to infiltrate French thought and were soon to exert, through the writings of Sartre and others, an influence critical of and inimical not only to religious attitudes but to traditional values all over the civilized world.

Although Le Senne was and saw himself as a conservative in philosophy, respectful of the idealist tradition, he kept vivaciously abreast of contemporary developments. Trained at a time when Bergson and Hamelin were much admired in France, he became more and more convinced that authentic philosophy consists in the relation of humanity with the Absolute, which is expressed in religious language as God. He saw philosophy, therefore, as having two poles: on the one side the Absolute as the focus of infinite value; on the other that same value as it is diffracted in human relations and human quests into the categories of truth, beauty, goodness, and love, producing manifestations as diverse and as complex as are human situations themselves.

To such a position in which none could be more sharply opposed to the fashionable trend toward positivism and linguistic analysis, Le Senne firmly held; yet he did not by any means dismiss such fashionable tendencies without examining them with some care and he certainly did not entirely repudiate existentialism as such, seeing it indeed at the heart of the French philosophical tradition. So he could engage in friendly cooperation with Gabriel Marcel, whose form of existentialism recognized and celebrated the values he cherished and which he saw in the thought of great French thinkers of the past, such as Descartes, Malebranche, Maine de Biran, Bergson, and Hamelin.

He was no mere conservator of an intellectual tradition of the past but, rather, a fearless champion of a philosophical position that was becoming increasingly unpopular. He was fully prepared to hold it against the stream of contemporary opinion. The respect his intellectual honesty won for him among the best of his colleagues was enhanced by the affection that his magnanimous personality could not fail to evoke.

Le courage, c'est le coeur de la morale,

By the time I met René Le Senne I was in my mid-thirties. I had already spent much time in France, having been an ardent francophile from the age of eleven. After I had finished my doctoral work at Oxford (completing, so I thought, all the degrees I should ever need or want), I was describing to a scholar at one of the provincial French universities the work I had been doing and my interest in pursuing further work on the relation of morality to religion and of doubt to faith. He urged me very strongly to meet René Le Senne, who was then professor of *morale* (ethics) at the Sorbonne, whom he believed to be more interested in my line of thought than would be most of the English moral philosophers of the day.

When eventually Le Senne invited me to take tea with him in his apartment in the rue César Franck one afternoon in 1946, he received me with a cordiality that was as elegant as it was unexpected from a Sorbonne professor to a complete stranger. He was a tall man, much taller than I had expected him to be, and of immensely impressive bearing. By this time he was in his middle sixties. His fine, aristocratic head was a shiny dome and on the lower part of his rather long upper lip was a white, neatly trimmed, hardly noticeable moustache, accentuating nevertheless his distinguished presence. He began at once to talk philosophy. Soon the conversation became animated. He brought out some of his own books, his *Traité de morale*, for instance, and his first book, *Introduction à la philosophie*, both substantial works. He mentioned that, although he could not speak English, he could read it quite easily. (He never uttered a word of English in my presence.) He said he looked forward to reading my first book, then in the press but delayed because of difficulties in the aftermath of war.

As the conversation proceeded he suggested that I do the work I had in mind, writing it in French, and present it for the *grand doctorate* (higher doctorate) at the Sorbonne, the *doctorat d'Etat* (State doctorate). Aghast at the proposal, I replied that not only had I not thought of such an idea; it seemed to me that it would be too formidable an undertaking in a language other than my own. If I were to contemplate a higher doctorate at all, it would be better to do it at a British university where I should not have the added hurdle of writing it in French, much as I loved the language.

He brushed aside that objection with a passing compliment to my use of the language and went on to explain what would be involved: two dissertations, officially known as the *thèse principale* and the *thèse complémentaire*, colloquially known as the *grande thèse* and the *petite*. Apprehensively, I asked what size they would be respectively. Pointing to a comparatively slim volume on one of his shelves he said, "Voila la grande thèse," and then, with a twinkle in his eye, he grasped an enormous tome on the bottom shelf, saying, "Et voici la petite!"

Having smiled with him at this little piece of fun I pursued my questioning. He explained the difference between the *petit doctorat* and the *grand doctorat*. The former, he said required a jury of only three and was designed with foreigners in mind, being of little practical use in France, while the latter demanded a jury of five and the *soutenance* or defense was *beaucoup plus brutal*(much rougher).[1] The minimum time for the *soutenance*, which of course would be entirely in French, would be five hours, since each member of the jury was expected to take at least the full hour allotted to him and, if they were *bavards* (talkative) as he said was likely, they could easily make it go on for seven or even eight.

I balked again. Even in my native tongue such an ordeal would be fearsome; by the seventh hour in French I might sound like a gibbering idiot. This objection, too, he brushed aside with further praise of my French diction, encouraging me with the reflection that the word *encouragement* itself came from *courage*, the heart (coeur) of morality. Le Senne was not only an optimist by temperament; his whole philosophy was grounded in an optimistic view of the world. His God seemed very much what Pascal called *le Dieu des philosophes et des savants* (the God of philosophers and scholars), yet he often said of Pascal: *il est très grand* (he is *very* great).

Then Madame Le Senne entered with tea and we talked of everyday things. After bidding my gracious host and hostess goodbye, I soon found myself outside in the avenue de Suffren. What a great man he was, I reflected. My thoughts turned to my early training in French when I had been warned to be careful where to put the adjective: *un grand homme* is not the same as *un homme grand*. Le Senne, I mused was both, so that I could put the adjective where I liked.

He was a Catholic both formally and by instinct, but he was anything other than fanatical about it. Much more philosopher than theologian, he admired thinkers such as Maurice Blondel and Gabriel Marcel more than, say, Jacques Maritain, whom he thought too tied to the scholastic tradition. He did admire Gilson's historical scholarship but often reminded me that he was more historian of philosophy than original thinker. His openness was sometimes startling. "If you are baptized," he said to me once, "you are a Catholic."

Some people called Le Senne a *demi-existentialiste* (half-existentialist), as they also called Marcel, but Le Senne disavowed this and claimed to be unashamedly an idealist in philosophy. He had no sympathy at all with those who opposed the notion of metaphysics (by that time almost every philosopher in the English-speaking world) while he had a kindly tolerance for anyone engaged in a metaphysical quest, even when the thought was far from his own, so long as the quest was pursued with intellectual honesty and skill. Nor had he much interest in Thomism. It was all right, he once said to me, for the theological seminaries, but *laissez-le dans les séminaires* (leave it in the seminaries)! His intellectual position was close to that of Louis Lavelle, with whom he collaborated in various scholarly enterprises. He was above all *un homme spirituel*, a strictly untranslatable adjective conveying a notion that goes far beyond both faith and intellect, beyond both culture and civilization. To me all this was immensely refreshing. I had already become disenchanted with the growing analytical tendency of philosophy in the English-speaking world, a tendency which, useful as it can be, was then in a somewhat brash phase.

For five years and more Le Senne kept up an astonishing correspondence with me, undeterred by his own busy life. Whenever I was in Paris we saw each other.

So lavish was his expenditure of time on me that I once expressed my embarrassment as well as my gratitude. "You need not thank me," he insisted. "All that comes within my function as a professor at the Sorbonne, which does not exclude sympathy." In fact, however, he would not have known how to restrict himself to the formal minimum of a duty, even if he could have wished to do so.

In ethical matters he was rigorous. I recall an occasion on which there was a temporary coffee shortage in France. I promised to bring him a pound or two on my next visit. He agreed on the condition that I must let him pay for it. I hardly expected that, when I brought him the coffee (a meagre gift indeed for one who had bestowed so many kindnesses on me), he would insist, as he did, not only on keeping the terms agreed upon but on working out the exact equivalent in francs to the third decimal place! He plainly wished that even in so small a matter we must avoid every hint, however slight, of bribery or corruption in our relationship.

Le Senne had guided many famous thinkers, some whose thought differed widely from his own. That profound genius Simone Weil, for example, one of the most remarkable Frenchwomen of the century, had worked under his guidance before her untimely death in 1943, three years before I met him. He spoke only occasionally of her and of others who had fallen under his influence in one way or another.

He collected stamps and I contributed now and then a few British and American ones to his collection. Significantly, however, he disavowed that his philately could be called a mere hobby. He pursued it, he insisted, to show his grandchildren the value and importance of family life. Stamps, when purchased for postage, are trivial in value, but in fifty years or more their value often increases enormously. Through philately, he believed, his grandchildren would find a practical lesson in the meaning and importance of family life, with all the moral riches it entails.

In his study, on the right side of the wall opposite the entrance, was an oil painting of Descartes. Among his favorite thinkers in the French tradition, apart from Pascal, were Maine de Biran (to whose spiritual humanism he felt close), Blondel, and Hamelin. Among thinkers in other countries he especially admired Josiah Royce in America and the English Unitarian thinker, James Martineau. But it was his intellectual openness that I most admired. He was extraordinarily learned. There were few philosophers, German or English or American, of whom he did not know a great deal, but if I happened to know of and mentioned anyone who had not come to his notice he eagerly sought to know more about him.

Now and then he would propose a walk in Paris, which I always enjoyed and from which I never failed to profit. He delighted to take me to lesser known museums and other places of interest, where he poured out the cornucopia of his knowledge of Old Paris, another of his hobbies. When we entered churches he behaved respectfully, of course, but I noticed that he did not, for instance, reverence the Sacrament. His attitude to the faith of his fathers was somewhat Hegelian: religion is important; it should be encouraged; but it is only a stage in development, leading to a deeper philosophical awareness. He seemed to think of religion, as did Hegel, as a sort of baby philosophy; some might even say a baby theosophy.

Nevertheless, so far was he from decrying religion that he once mildly reproached me for seeming to have used the term "superstition" in a denigrating way.

"Ah," he said, "you do not like superstition. Many Protestants do not like it. *Moi, je l'aime!* (*I like it!*)" His attitude was perhaps somewhat like that of Gandhi toward the idols of his Hindu religion: he would not use idols himself, but he would defend to the death the right of others to use them if idols were in any way helpful in their spiritual development.

In idealist fashion he saw all human values as a path to God, in whom he firmly believed. In his own way he was somewhat like Henri Bremond in the latter's adherence to a Salesian tradition of "devout humanism," antithetical to, for example, George Tyrrell. Le Senne took a metaphysical approach to everything. It was his whole life. Those who like myself had the privilege of knowing him well could be in no doubt that he lived what he taught. He lived his metaphysics as some live a religious faith. "I refuse to condemn reality," he once said, "on the ground that it includes, for instance, war. We are not made for rest but for creation." By that sort of utterance he meant that obstacles were put in our path to enable us to create values. In his work *Obstacle et valeur*, he contends that the creation of moral values is a response to difficulties and discouragements.

In his later years he became interested in what he called characterology. His thought in this field, expressed in the large work, *Traité de caractérologie*, was warmly received by many and won him friends outside the academic world, but it also evoked much hostility both from some of his colleagues in philosophy and from empirical psychologists who questioned the value and even the validity of his results. His characterology, however, may be regarded as an outgrowth if not a corollary of his basic metaphysical stance. It reflected both his passionate humanism and his deep confidence in the fundamental goodness of the universe.

Le Senne always minimized the importance of honors that came to himself. Monseigneur Louis de Raeymaeker, Vice-Rector of the University of Louvain, once told me that Le Senne, when he gave a public lecture at Louvain, was very nervous. No doubt that would have sprung from his innate respect for the Church, with which that university is so closely allied. At any rate, Louvain made him a doctor *honoris causa*. A year or so later he was elected a *membre de l'Institut de France*. While he was typing a few lines to facilitate my own work at the Bibliothèque Nationale, I congratulated him. He glanced up very momentarily, a slight smile on his fine countenance. "It is something that comes with the loss of hair," he joked. I said I knew people who had lost their hair but were not members of the Institut. He merely continued to smile and paid no further attention.

He was constantly introducing me to books and people. He even introduced me to the French ambassador at the Court of Saint James, Monsieur Massigli, on the offchance that the ambassador might be helpful to me at some time. But he admitted, characteristically, that it is often better to know the sergeant than the general.

When, five years after our first meeting, the time approached when I should have to defend my two theses in French before the jury of five, I again voiced my apprehension about the length of the ordeal. "On one point I can help," he said. "Since I shall be president of the jury, it is my privilege to choose the date. I shall choose the thirteenth of July. It is impossible to keep any Frenchman very late on the *veille du Quatorze* (eve of Bastille Day). The *soutenance* will not last more than the minimum of five hours." He added that he planned to arrange that it should be, if at all possible, in the Salle Liard, a magnificent gilded audience chamber.

The custom prevails at the Sorbonne, or did at that time, requiring a candidate for the *grand doctorat* to make a social call on each of the five members of the jury within the ten days immediately preceding the *soutenance*. I found this a most charming arrangement. My jury for the *grande thèse* consisted of Le Senne, Emile Souriau, and Pierre-Maxime Schuhl. For the *petite thèse* it was Henri Gouhier, who later became a member of the Académie Française, and Emile Pons. At these social meetings all received me with the utmost courtesy. We talked about anything other than my work and the forthcoming ordeal. The idea was simply that we should meet socially before it occurred. Some offered tea, others wine. Schuhl, a bachelor of forty-nine, received me in his elegant apartment, Monsieur et Madame Pons in their suburban home in Châtenay-Malabry.

On the appointed day, July 13, 1951, at 1:30 PM, I duly appeared, of course, at the Salle Liard. That beautiful hall is adorned with very large portraits of the great men in French letters: Pascal, Racine, and the like, and gazing down from behind the jury's dais is that of Cardinal Richelieu, founder of the French Academy. The jury's dais was high above me. The five of them sat at a semicircular table covered with green cloth, while I sat on a somewhat rickety chair far below. Outsiders, sometimes a fairly large crowd of them, had come to witness the spectacle, some out of interest in the subject, many out of curiosity, some through lack of anything better to do. Had it not been for the graceful conduct of the jury and the high respect with which they treated me throughout the long proceedings, I could well have felt singularly like a worm with the eyes of all turned upon it.

Le Senne had thoughtfully given me a rundown on the character and temperament of the men I should be facing. He had told me, for instance, that Pons would probably begin by saying, *"Moi, je ne suis pas philosophe."* [2] That was precisely how he did begin. Souriau was perhaps the least sympathetic to my thought, but all were most courteous.

First, I had to give a twenty-minute oral account of the thesis I was defending. Each member of the jury in turn then began with a brief appreciation, glided almost imperceptibly into a critique, then less imperceptibly into specific questions. There was a coffee break of fifteen minutes with the announcement that the *soutenance* would resume at precisely the end of that period, according to the clock in the room. I fled to a café in the rue Soufflot, with a dear young friend, André Michel, now both a retired professeur de lycée and an accomplished writer in Paris, and consumed the blackest coffee I have ever drunk in my life. At 6:30 PM the *soutenance* was declared over. The jury retired to deliberate, as at a murder trial, and then I stood as they reentered to pronounce their verdict, which was that I had been found worthy, *mention très honorable* (summa cum laude).

A little official from the office suddenly appeared with a tiny note to the effect that I must come to the office the following week, pay a small sum of money and receive the university diploma. When I went, the diploma was awaiting me, but since one gets two diplomas, one from the University of Paris and the other a much grander one from the Republic of France, I asked when I might expect to receive the latter. The little clerk looked at me through beady eyes. Thinking I knew

French bureaucracy, I joked, "I suppose it will take months?"
He paused. "Years," he said laconically. "*Ah, vous blaguez,*"[3] I said
incredulously. "It could not possibly take years."
He thought again, as if counting. "Six years," he said with
decisiveness. "It is impossible," I persisted, forgetting that *impossible
n'est pas français.* (So the French express the power of positive
thinking.)

With a sigh he patiently went on to explain at considerable length
how carefully he had done his computation. The petition would have
to be signed by the Minister of Education, who is of course a very busy
man. Naturally it would go through channels. In the course of its
travels it would pass over the desks of two classes of people: (1) those
whose occupants would be overworked and therefore unable to attend
to the petition for possibly as long as three weeks, and (2) those whose
occupants would have nothing to do and who therefore would be
delighted to have the petition to adorn their desks and who certainly
would hold on to it at least till some other work arrived, which might
well take three weeks or more.

As he talked, he never smiled or blinked an eye. He merely looked a
little bored as though I ought to be intelligent enough to know all these
things without having to elicit a full explanation in detail. As he went
on and on my incredulity diminished and I began to be half persuaded
that it might take as much as three years.

"Well then, what about the other three years?" I asked. He
continued the stony stare and the unsmiling countenance as he replied,
"Monsieur, twice three is six. The petition that has taken three years to
reach its destination, the Minister of Education, must come back by the
same channels as it went to him."

In the course of the next few years, I was in Paris several times and
each time I called on someone such as the Dean of the Faculty of
Letters or a secretary, to inquire about my state diploma. No
satisfaction. At length, I asked Le Senne himself, who merely said,
"Why do you want a diploma? If you ever had to prove you are a
docteur-ès-lettres you would do so from the Gazette, not by means of
diploma." Then he added, "Come to think of it, I don't believe I ever
got mine." He was now seventy and had become *docteur-ès-lettres* at
forty-nine.

Eventually I had decided to forget the whole thing, but it happened
that one morning in 1957 I was in Paris again with my wife. I asked her
what she felt inclined to do on our first morning there. She mentioned
that she had not been in the Latin Quarter for a long time. Perhaps we
might go there?

A bright idea occurred to me. "Let's go and see about the famous

diploma," I suggested. "It will be an objective—something to do." We
did. And it had just come in. I looked at the calendar. It was July 13,
1957, precisely six years to the day. That little clerk knew his job.
Other countries, as they grow old and tired, fall into the toils of
bureaucracy. In France, however, it is a fine art. It might be
conceivable that a diploma could take six years in Germany or Italy, in
England or the United States, but only in France could it be delivered
promptly to a six-year delivery date. For in France the delay is due to
neither dilatoriness nor procrastination, both alien to the ethos of the
French people and far removed from the vitality of the French temper.
When France takes six years to produce a diploma there must be a
good reason for it. At any rate, it makes sense within bureaucratic
logic.

To Le Senne, however, bureaucracy, like everything else in the
nonspiritual, mechanistic order, was merely an obstacle, a hurdle to be
surmounted. Francophile though I am, I doubt if I could ever have
adequately appreciated the true greatness of France had not I had the
good fortune to have met René Le Senne, to have imbibed his thought,
and to have enjoyed his uniquely moral and spiritual personality. For
although I have known many French people and loved many of those I
have known, I have never met one I admired more than René Le Senne.
He often reminded me that if France were *la fille aînée de l'Eglise et son
epée* (the eldest daughter of the Church and her sword), it was so only
by accident, since history might well have taken a very different turn.
He personally combined the expansive charm of the *ancien régime* with
a Hebraic zeal for justice and a Stoic sense of moral rectitude. In men
and women of this calibre lies the true greatness of France.

After the death of Le Senne in 1954, I had the honor of being asked
to write a *témoignage* (a personal tribute) in *Les Etudes Philosophiques*,
published by the Presses Universitaires de France, the original text of
which is reproduced here, summing up succinctly the impressions I
have described in this chapter.

TÉMOIGNAGE

Il y a longtemps que j'ai appris, dans mon enfance en Écosse,
qu'il n'existe pas en anglais de traduction exacte du mot français
« spirituel » ; mais je n'en ai appris le sens exact, qu'après avoir fait
la connaissance de René Le Senne, qui était, avant tout, un homme
spirituel, aussi bien qu'un homme de l'esprit. Ce qui provoque chez
moi la plus grande admiration, c'est l'intégration de sa pensée et de
sa vie. Sensible aux obstacles que rencontre le philosophe qui voudrait
pénétrer, si peu que ce fût, le mystère de l'existence, rien ne pouvait
le décourager de la recherche de la valeur, qui donne son caractère
mystérieux à la vie humaine, et qui indique la destinée personnelle
de l'homme. La conscience qu'il avait des obstacles qu'apporte l'expé-
rience n'était point limitée par sa confiance en la valeur qui doit les

surmonter. « Que l'on coupe mon téléphone, écrit-il, cela ne prouve pas que l'homme avec lequel je téléphonais est anéanti. »

De mon point de vue d'étranger, francophile, j'ai trouvé en René Le Senne, qui était également sympathique à la piété religieuse délicate de l'Ancien Régime et à l'idéal de liberté qui se cache et se révèle à la fois dans la Révolution, un symbole immortel de toute la civilisation française, sans laquelle notre monde serait si pauvre.

Si généreuse était sa manière de penser, qu'il pouvait à peine comprendre l'étroitesse de la plupart des hommes. C'est un peu là, me semble-t-il, ce qui le porta vers la caractérologie. Son humilité d'esprit s'accordait parfaitement à son éloquence vigoureuse. Un an après que l'Université de Louvain l'eut fait docteur *honoris causa*, il fut élu membre de l'Institut de France ; je le félicitais alors que, devant sa machine à écrire, il tapait quelques lignes pour faciliter mon propre travail à la Bibliothèque Nationale. Levant les yeux, il essaya de réprimer l'ardeur de mes félicitations. « C'est ce qui vient avec la perte des cheveux », plaisanta-t-il. C'était toujours ainsi qu'il minimisait la générosité tout à fait extraordinaire avec laquelle, pendant de longues années, il s'est mis sans contrainte à ma disposition. « Vous n'avez pas à me remercier », avait-il l'habitude de me dire. « Tout cela rentre dans mes fonctions de professeur à la Sorbonne, qui n'excluent pas la sympathie. » A vrai dire, René Le Senne avait un esprit si généreux qu'il n'aurait pas su se borner au minimum d'un devoir, même s'il avait pu y songer.

La première fois que je l'ai rencontré personnellement, en 1946, dans son appartement de Paris, je le trouvais, à ma surprise, plus grand que je ne m'y attendais. Dans la conversation animée qui suivit, je lui ai confié les doutes que j'éprouvais sur ma capacité de rédiger en français deux longues thèses pour le doctorat d'état, et de soutenir celles-ci dans cette langue, pendant cinq ou six heures, devant un jury de Sorbonne. Se mettant tout de suite à m'encourager, il m'a parlé alors, d'une manière caractéristique, de l'idée de courage, le « cœur » de la morale. Pendant une heure, nous avons parlé de métaphysique, lui avec l'ardeur d'un homme qui discute la chose la plus précieuse de sa vie. Puis, après l'entrée de Mme Le Senne, avec qui nous avons pris le thé, la conversation s'est dirigée vers des sujets plus légers, et il conserva là cette même vivacité qui m'avait enchanté dans sa conversation métaphysique. Enfin, leur ayant fait mes adieux, je me suis bientôt trouvé dans l'avenue de Suffren, où mes réflexions se sont tournées encore une fois vers mon enfance en Écosse : l'on m'y avait appris qu'il ne fallait pas confondre les locutions françaises, « grand homme » et « homme grand » ! C'était avec une satisfaction particulière que je me disais que, dans le cas de René Le Senne, au moins, on pouvait placer l'adjectif n'importe où !

NINE

Martin D'Arcy

Martin Cyril D'Arcy (1888-1976) was born in Bath, the fourth and youngest son of a barrister. The family was of Irish and, more remotely, Norman descent, with here and there a coronet in the family tree. From school at Stonyhurst he went off to the Jesuit novitiate at Roehampton in 1906, back to Stonyhurst for further studies in 1909, and thence to Oxford with a small, elite group of Jesuit scholastics sent thither by their Society. At Oxford Martin D'Arcy found his intellectual home. Although in Moderations he took only a second class, from there on his Oxford career was brilliant, with not only a first in Greats but several of the most prestigious prizes and other awards.

In 1916 he went back to Stonyhurst to teach. Father Francis Hannan, who had been one of his pupils there, reports that his teaching was of special quality: he almost never obtruded opinions of his own but forced the boys to go to sources and form their own opinions. He would prescribe, for instance, two essays to be written by two boys, the one defending Gladstone, the other Disraeli. Sometimes he would demand an essay on a subject on which no outside source could be available, such as "On being yourself." He would test powers of observation by calling for an essay on the difference between a good portrait and a good photograph. For English boys at a Jesuit school in those days, such teaching methods must have been novel and certainly invigorating to the young minds under his charge.

After the usual further studies prescribed in the long Jesuit training, he was eventually ordained priest in 1921 and admitted to solemn profession in the Order on February 2, 1926. In 1927, he returned to Oxford. There and in London he began to make a name for himself for his remarkable combination of intellectual energy and personal conviction, of careful scholarship and originality of thought.

In 1932, he became master of Campion Hall, Oxford, then in 1945 English Provincial (head of the Jesuit order in England), a position he held till 1950, when he was removed by Rome.

The author of numerous books, some of them well known and admired far beyond Catholic audiences, he received many invitations to the United States. He grew to love America, made many friends, and received honorary degrees from several universities, including Georgetown, Fordham, and Marquette. In 1956, he was elected a Fellow of the Royal Society of Literature and, in 1960, a foreign member of the American Academy of Arts and Sciences.

He was strikingly distinctive both in appearance and in personality, and gathered to his large circle of interesting friends some of the most celebrated men and women of the time in literature, painting, and drama. Among these, Augustus John, Evelyn Waugh, Alec Guinness, and the Sitwells are but a few examples. But Campion Hall was the focus of his life. It was there that he built up a collection of works of sacred art (vestments, chalices, paintings, sculptures) that Oxford wits called *objets D'Arcy*.

Rather a pooh Gainsbruh, don't you think?

Father D'Arcy was like no other Jesuit, indeed like no other man on earth. The Jesuits have an inbuilt paradox: the product of a romantic sixteenth-century Spanish tradition of chivalry and military discipline calculated to crush individualism, they have succeeded in producing some of the most remarkable individualists in the Church. This individualism is sometimes attributed to the Renaissance spirit that the Society of Jesus has inherited in contrast to both the ancient monastic orders and the medieval friars. A society of clerics regular (neither friars nor monks nor secular priests), they have been notoriously ingenious and successful in regularizing irregularities in the interpretation of their own rule. If they had not existed, surely Pascal or some other master of Christian paradox would have had to invent them. No one, however, could have invented the superlatively improbable Father D'Arcy.

Because of my interest in the topics of some of his announced talks when I was at Oxford, I went to hear him more than once before actually meeting him. He was fiftyish at the time and looked like a figure out of an El Greco painting: dark, thin, emaciated, with piercing eyes and long, tentacle-like fingers that seemed now and then to be playing an unseen piano. In those days he wore his gray hair unfashionably long, in delicate little ringlets. (Twenty years later, when men had begun wearing their hair long, he had his cut short.) His smile was a diabolical grin and his demeanor highly aristocratic. He looked as though he had come straight out of the Gunpowder Plot and had successfully emerged as Master of Campion Hall, the position he then held at Oxford. Both very English and very Ultramontane Catholic, he almost constantly gave the impression that anything not both of these was too vulgar to merit serious attention.

The University of Oxford consists of a number of colleges, some very ancient and others much more recent, that together constitute the University; but private houses of study at Oxford have grown up from time to time to meet special needs without their gaining recognition as integral units of the university. Such a house had been opened under license in 1896 to enable Jesuits to live and study at Oxford in their own community and under the guidance of their own teachers. Under a statute of 1918, it received official recognition as having the status of a "permanent private hall" and such was its status when Father D'Arcy was appointed to head it.

It was at Campion Hall, where some young Jesuit friends of mine had invited me to tea towards the end of his period as Master, that I was introduced to him. We were looking at some of the paintings he had collected, in particular one that had not yet been hung but was standing on the floor. It was a picture over which another had been painted and subsequently removed, revealing a seventeenth-century Italian painting of the Holy Family in vivid colors: what might perhaps be called a pictorial palimpsest.

I was gazing intently at this painting when Father D'Arcy strode magnificently toward us. When formal introduction had been made, he remarked at my interest and said with some pride, "Picked it up in a Lancashire farmhouse. A pastoral scene with cows on it. Paid five pounds for it. This is what we found underneath."

Showing my appreciation for the work, I mentioned that I had noticed a very odd thing: our Lady had a halo, Joseph had a halo, but our Lord had none. He stared down at the picture for so long and, as if not believing his own eyes, that I felt I had to say something. With a mischievous smile, I ventured, "Isn't that carrying Trent a little too far, Father?"

He gave me a withering look and said icily, "Bless my soul, so he hasn't," and strode off with sinister *hauteur*. Later, however, he was affably showing me some of the treasures of the sacristy. He gently pulled out a drawer, fumbled slightly with the vestments in it and said,

"Mm, nothing much there—just some eighteenth-century Spanish chasubles."

Having paused for dramatic effect he then pulled out another drawer and said, "Well, here *is* something rather interesting: a fifteenth-century Portuguese dalmatic. Rather fine, don't you think?"

Where he picked up all his marvelous *trouvailles* I cannot tell. They could not all have come from Lancashire farmhouses, which are not on the whole very likely depositories of Portuguese dalmatics. In any case, although I seemed to be in a Jesuit Ali Baba's cave, none of the treasures even remotely compared with the Master himself.

For all the Englishness of his manner, he was more Keltic than Saxon in temper. I once attended a debate at Pusey House in which he and the rotund Trevor Jalland of Magdalen undertook to cross swords. The room was packed with undergraduates eager to see fur fly. Dr. Jalland, a very learned Anglican, gave a long, careful, workmanlike historical survey, which Father D'Arcy followed with a delightfully debonair and witty exposition that bore little relation to Jalland's speech but was pleasanter to the ear and revelatory of a different kind of erudition.

At question time, a very young woman, probably a freshman, raised a query, no doubt in all innocence, about Pope Honorius, directing it specifically to Father D'Arcy. Father D'Arcy, who somehow always looked as though he were about to empty into one's tea the contents of a venom ring personally handed down as an heirloom from the Borgias, apparently suspected a deep-dyed ecclesiastical plot to catch him out, glared fiercely at the poor girl and said imperiously something to the effect that he had little interest in such traditional controversies and would prefer that Dr. Jalland answer the question. Jalland duly did, meticulously going over the ground with never a smile or a frown.

In the end, one had the impression of watching a struggle between an Anglican lion and a Jesuit boa constrictor that had gone hungry for weeks in anticipation. Father D'Arcy somehow always looked hungry.

Oxford could boast many charming eccentrics in those days; nevertheless, the sight of Father D'Arcy and Edith Sitwell (one of his many distinguished converts) walking down the High together was perhaps the most startling *tableau vivant*. Back in those days I once encountered him on top of an Edinburgh bus in animated conversation with a rough sort of character, possibly an old Irish laborer. I exchanged some conversation with him before he and his companion descended at Lauriston Street, the dingy location of the soot-blackened Jesuit church dedicated to the Sacred Heart. If you knew Father D'Arcy at all, you were never surprised by the places in which or the persons with whom you might chance to find him. Still, I suspect there was always something unusual or special about anybody with whom he willingly consorted, because in Father D'Arcy's eyes pedestrianism was absolutely the only unforgivable sin. He had the utmost charity toward all sinners and could bear gladly with all vices and every frailty of man or woman except mediocrity.

When Father D'Arcy left Oxford in 1945 to become English provincial (head of the English Province of the Order), men were returning in droves from service in World War II. The Jesuit novitiate was crowded in a way that those accustomed to conditions today would find almost incredible. Much was expected of a Jesuit administrator called to such an important position in the Order at such a time in the world's history.

Father D'Arcy was by any reckoning no doubt less gifted as an administrator than as a scholar and writer. Nevertheless, he had a vision far beyond what could be seen in him by lesser men, who belittled it by privately jeering at what they saw only as his propensity for buying up old houses with Catholic associations. He had in fact an unusually keen eye for opportunities and a long-range understanding of the needs of the Society.

His administrative weakness lay perhaps chiefly in his tendency to neglect to seek the support of bishops and others in the hierarchy who are easily offended when they feel their authority sidestepped. This is especially true in the relation between the Roman Catholic hierarchy and the Jesuit Order whose special position in the Church has so often been a source of envy and jealousy on the part of bishops.

Father Vincent Turner, a colleague, who knew him particularly well, especially in his years at Campion Hall and in the Provincialate, has recorded in a contribution to the archives of the Order his testimony to Father D'Arcy's humane qualities (so important in intelligent administrative leadership) and concern for all aspects of the welfare of those under his care. "He gave everybody breathing space; he encouraged their initiatives and trusted them through thick and thin . . . . He treasured every spark of individuality." He also hated committees. His respect for individual work was too great to like to see it submerged in the inevitably pedestrian character of committee work.

The young Jesuits he taught were impressed above all by one quality in the Master—his courtesy. "We had never been treated like princelings before." He had the utmost respect for personal privacy. Any political views he ever expressed gave the impression of romantically extreme conservatism, yet he was unusually open to ideas, even those that accorded ill with his own temperament. In some quarters, he was suspected of snobbery, but he was certainly anything other than a snob in any vulgar sense. He was unashamedly elitist, for being above all a Christian humanist he felt that egalitarianism choked, if it did not destroy, the finest human values that he cherished so much and did so much to foster in all who came under his care.

Both in his mastership at Campion Hall and in the wider sphere of the provincialate, Father D'Arcy abundantly manifested the qualities that distinguish a great leader from a mere administrator. After five years as Provincial, however, his style of government had not found favor at Rome. Impatient with paperwork, distrustful of the Roman Curia, and perhaps also, despite his innate courtesy, disdainful of local bishops in whose dioceses he worked, he was not palatable to the run-of-the-mill bureaucrats in whom so much power is vested by the Church. In 1950, he was summarily dismissed by the Jesuit authorities in Rome, to the astonishment, not to say outrage, of his English associates.

According to Father Turner, the letter of dismissal cited three reasons: scamping of visitations to major houses of the Society in England, granting too much freedom (*nimia libertas*) to young priests, and general administrative neglect. The unfairness of this highhanded treatment of a man who, as Father Turner testifies, "loved the Society more than anything on earth" shocked those most intimately acquainted with his personality and his work. Although he did not publicly parade his grief, I suspect, as did many of his closest friends, that it broke his heart.

He was sixty-two at the time. During the remaining twenty-six years of his life both the Church and the world seemed to him to be taking retrograde steps, moving away from the kind of humanism he accounted so important for the welfare of both. He felt the values he had cherished most were eroding wherever he turned. Worst of all the Church and even the Society he so passionately loved, seemed to have betrayed their own nature. He had thought of them as essentially good, despite the inevitable minor stupidities and narrownesses that have always beset religious institutions. To what extent he was disillusioned no one can tell. I can only say that in his later years something was missing in him. Superficially he was still much the same. His affection for people, his sense of drama, his slightly impish asides, were all in a flourishing state of health. He still spoke for the Church, but no longer with quite the passionate zest of his earlier years.

Of course, one might attribute the change to old age, but those who knew him well knew better. He found much solace not only in the welcome accorded him by the various American universities and other institutions that invited him to lecture, but even more in the warm appreciation his appearance evoked in his audiences. What many of the students and others who attended them appreciated most was his obvious affection for people and his immensely interesting reminiscences of famous men and women whom he had met, for by this time his thought was no longer subject to much continuing development, although what it had been was brilliantly displayed in his mellowed personality. Both the portrait of him by Augustus John at Campion Hall (he had tutored that famous painter's son) and the fascinating mosaic of him in New York's Museum of Modern Art seemed to come to life before one's eyes as he talked, now of Lord Hailsham, now of the Sitwells, glowing with delight as he spoke and causing his audience to glow with him, less at those he talked about than at the way he talked about them.

After I went to live in the United States in 1949, Father D'Arcy disappeared entirely from my life for more than a decade. Then suddenly, he began reappearing. Now in his seventies, he was more El Greco than ever, yet at the same time considerably more mellow. In this later period I first reencountered him at a lecture he was giving in Los Angeles at which I was seated beside him, along with the ever-amiable Monsignor John Sheridan, whose spirit always exhaled the best of the soul of Ireland, and with Walter Starkie, an indefatigable lecturer and a prolific writer on Spain and the gypsies.

At this time I was a university dean. Since Father D'Arcy recalled our earlier meetings with pleasure, was obviously a delightful lecturer as well as a competent scholar, and much relished visits to the United States, I was glad to take the opportunity of helping to have him invited for various occasions at my own institution. He taught a course for us one summer in medieval philosophy and on other occasions gave scholarly and entertaining lectures.

The spirit of Vatican II was alien to his traditionalist outlook and he ill disguised, if he disguised at all, his lack of sympathy with its aims and his antipathy to some of its results. He talked of the Mass in the vernacular with as much relish as would a champagne vintner of railway station tea. To the obvious suggestion that it would nevertheless help many people to understand and appreciate the Mass better, he replied with a story in which he claimed to have known a scholarly and eccentric Anglican rector in England who preached for years in Attic Greek to his congregation of yokels. Asked why they did not revolt, Father D'Arcy said, "Oh, they rather enjoyed it. They wouldn't have understood him any better in English."

His many gifts did not include any very practical bent. No doubt he had accustomed himself to leaving everyday matters to devoted and willing helpers. Nevertheless, he was often eager to show his willingness to undertake the lowliest of tasks. During one of his visits to California in the sixties, I proposed a trip to an interesting Benedictine foundation some eighty miles away. One of his many devoted admirers volunteered to drive us and off we went through rather hot desert country till the radiator water was literally boiling. We noticed a trickling stream far below the road and were discussing how to get a utensil of some sort to carry water.

Suddenly, we observed that Father D'Arcy had vanished. Some minutes later he hove into sight carrying in his battered black felt hat a few thimblefuls of water—all that remained after he had made the steep ascent. He was quite disappointed that the result of his labors was of no use, nor did I make matters any better by quoting Kant, a thinker he had been long trained to suspect: nothing is good without qualification except a good will. My wife did much better by pointing out to him that his now dripping wet clerical hat would provide protection from the hot sun. At the priory, however, he completely recovered his composure and insisted on going immediately to Vespers which, I was able to assure him, were still, at that time, in Latin.

Even in his later years, his mellowing notwithstanding, he had still a strong vein of mischief in him. We took him to the Huntington Library in San Marino. The treasures there include a Gutenberg Bible, the Ellesmere Chaucer, and many other priceless manuscripts, as well as beautiful oriental gardens and a fine art collection with an emphasis on eighteenth-century English paintings and French furniture. One of the most famous of the paintings is Gainsborough's *Blue Boy* which thousands of eager spectators have oohed and aahed over every day for decades.

Father D'Arcy, always a distinguished figure whose clerical garb was so much a part of him that it seemed almost as though it were his very skin, gazed sphinx-like at the painting, peered into it, stood back from it, then in a shrill English voice that resounded throughout the main gallery, remarked to his entourage, "Rather a pooh Gainsbruh, don't you think?"

I am sure he thought no such thing, but he did love to shock people, especially if he thought them guilty of pretending to enjoy what their pedestrian taste could not equip them to appreciate. The culture vultures in their turn could hardly have been more dazed had they seen painters arriving in the Sistine Chapel to redo the ceiling. Father D'Arcy, unostentatiously savoring the effect of his words, then retreated with quiet glee to another gallery. He seemed pleased with the success of his missionary labors, through which he hoped to lead people to see that, in art as in religion, it is all right to fly with eagles or waddle with ducks, but if you are anywhere in between you had better shut up.

One evening while he was dining at our home, my wife happened to ask him about his Stonyhurst days, which elicited nostalgic memories. He recalled student songs such as *Gaudeamus igitur*. I tried out what I could remember of the songs of my own youth and came up with lines from *Laudiger Horatius*:

> *Quid juvat aeternitas nominis amare*
> *Nisi terrae filias licet et potare?*[1]

"That one was not in our repertoire," he said primly, quaffing his wine and changing to another topic of conversation.

Although Father D'Arcy's name is widely associated with his influence in the conversion of interesting and distinguished men and women, the fact that they were interesting and distinguished did not obtrude itself in his recounting of circumstances attending their reception into the Church. After all, since Aristotle's God draws to himself all things without even moving, it seemed to Father D'Arcy by no means surprising that Holy Church should draw to herself people of discriminating taste.

Dame Edith Sitwell was one of these. Father D'Arcy liked to tell of that Thursday, August 4, 1955, when she was received into the Church according to the customary rites, which took place in the Ignatius Chapel at the Jesuit House in Farm Street. Alec Guinness was already in the chapel when Father D'Arcy, Evelyn Waugh, and other friends proceeded thither to await her arrival. Dame Edith eventually strode in about noon, attired in one of her highly original costumes, giving her the air of a Spanish grandee of about the time of Ignatius Loyola, although she was of course as English as the cliffs of Dover. (Like her brother Sir Osbert, who used to list himself as "educated during the holidays from Eton," Dame Edith could be counted on never to do anything in a pedestrian way.) Father Philip Caraman, another notable Jesuit contemporary whom Father D'Arcy had known from Stonyhurst days, was also present.

Dame Edith, having duly received conditional baptism, disappeared into the confessional to make her peace with God and the Church. The benisons soon over, Father D'Arcy, Waugh, Guinness, and others repaired to the Sesame, Dame Edith's club in Grosvenor Street, where she entertained them to a luncheon that Father D'Arcy described as elegant, although, characteristically, he never could quite remember what they ate except that there seemed to be a lot of lobster and copious draughts of wine.

The influence of America on the later part of Father D'Arcy's life was enormous. It was in New York that he met Teilhard de Chardin. In California, Aldous Huxley invited him to his home in Pacific Palisades.

Of that association there, I have received dramatic accounts of Huxley naked in a mud bath and Father D'Arcy alongside in full clerical dress. Truman Capote also knew him. At Princeton's Institute of Advanced Studies, Edmund Wilson and Father D'Arcy shared a kitchen. Neither could cook and both lived pretty much out of cans. Father D'Arcy was the sort of man who, while he immensely appreciated the finest cuisine, could survive on iron rations. Neither regimen could ever have made the slightest difference to his spare figure. He looked as lean and hungry after a sumptuous banquet as ever he could have looked in an Athonite Lent. Perhaps in culinary as in all other tastes, he found the best and the worst more congenial than the mediocrity in between.

Unique as was his personality, his greatest influence on people accustomed to serious thought on religious matters came through his prolific writings. Among these the book by which he came to be most widely known beyond as well as within Roman Catholic circles is probably *The Mind and Heart of Love*, a profoundly sensitive study of the nature of love in all its aspects. *The Nature of Belief* was also important in its day. In *No Absent God*, he addressed himself in his always special way to a classic concept in religious phenomenology: that God may be better known through his absence than through his presence. But his range of topics was wide and in all of them his treatment reflects his own highly individualist way of interpreting a very traditionalist understanding of Catholic thought.

All of his writings exhibit, as in a more intimate way did his conversation, a peculiarly mystical *genre* of the Catholic spirit. Yet he could not be said to be mystical in any generally accepted sense of the term. He was far too traditionalist for that. His spirituality was distinctly his own. The discipline gave him an iron resolve and sustained his intense loyalty to the Church; his flair came from a creative spirit within him that seemed to prosper in the particular mix of soil in which he had been nurtured. In any other, it might have died.

Some would call him, no doubt, a hothouse plant that would have withered fast outside the rich soil and warm sunshine of his Catholic heritage, bereft of the morning dew of the Mass, but that would be to misunderstand Martin D'Arcy. There was no spiritual humidity in him at all. He was more like a desert flower than a tropical plant. He always looked as parched as a tree in drought, as lonely as the lone cypress in Monterey, yet he seemed to carry within him wherever he went just enough sustenance to take him to the next Catholic oasis. He was indeed somewhat like a camel, both in his endurance and in his pride; but the pride lay more in his sense of spiritual heritage than in personal accomplishment.

If it be true, as I think it is, that a man's character may best be seen in the kind of person he admires, then for an understanding of D'Arcy we should look to Gerard Manley Hopkins (1844-1889), for whom he had a profound admiration and on whom he was an expert. Hopkins, whose poetry displays great intensity of feeling and a freedom of rhythm uncharacteristic of his day, as well as marked individualism in his use of words, exercised considerable influence posthumously over other poets; yet during his life his poetic genius had been hardly recognized at all beyond an intimate circle of friends. He was a friend of Robert Bridges, who, having been the pupil, at Balliol, of the great Benjamin Jowett, became Poet Laureate in 1913. Coming under the influence of Pusey and others in the Oxford Movement, Hopkins eventually became a Roman Catholic in 1866 and was admitted two years later to the Jesuit novitiate. Ordained priest in 1877, he was appointed Professor of Greek at Dublin in 1884, which chair he held till his death. Father D'Arcy found in Hopkins an ideal. He was easily persuaded to give readings of the poetry of Hopkins and when he did so his own personality seemed to glow as if he had come in from a cold, dreary walk to a warm fireside at home.

Father Edward Yarnold writes of the last twenty-six years of D'Arcy's life as "something of a protracted dark night. It was not only that he had a deep sense of failure, perhaps even of injustice, over his curtailed provincialate. He felt almost totally out of sympathy with the passing of the England he had loved before the war, and with the changes in the Church. The particular idea of Christian humanism, which had sprung from his heart and his soul and which he had expounded in all his writings, seemed to be discarded not only by his country but by his Church. By the end he ceased to conceal the fact that he looked forward to death." Yet as Father Francis Edwards testifies in a letter to me, "Only in the last year or two of his life did his natural verve and vivacity begin to fail."

The end came on November 20, 1976, at the hospital of Saints John and Elizabeth in London where, ironically, Father Corbishley, who had succeeded him in the mastership of Campion Hall in 1945, had died a few months earlier. Requiem Mass was celebrated on November 29, 1976, with Cardinal Archbishop Hume as the principal concelebrant. Father Frederick Copleston delivered an address, printed in *Month*, January, 1977. Another requiem was celebrated at Oxford later at the University Chaplaincy, not at Campion Hall because the numbers attending were too large to be accommodated there, and Lord Hailsham delivered an address that was published in the *Tablet*, February 19, 1977. Father D'Arcy was buried in Kensal Green, sharing a grave with Father Martindale, a notable Jesuit contemporary. In the words of Martial's epigram, let us say *sit tibi terra levis*: may the earth lie light upon you! And let us add, of course the ancient Catholic prayer, *et lux perpetua luceat ei*: and let light perpetual shine upon him. Even on this earth the light he shed was as special as was his mercurial mind.

Martin D'Arcy

TEN

Arthur Marder

Arthur Jacob Marder (1910-1980) was born in Boston and received his undergraduate education at Harvard, where, also, he was graduated Ph.D. in 1936. From Harvard, he went to the University of Oregon as assistant professor of history. Then, after some research positions that included one with the OSS (1941-2) and a year of teaching at Hamilton College, he received an appointment at the University of Hawaii in 1944. He remained there till 1964, leaving with the rank of senior professor of history to become professor of history at the University of California at Irvine, the position he held on his retirement in 1977. He was a member of numerous professional societies, including the American Philosophical Society, as well as the American Academy of Arts and Sciences, Phi Beta Kappa, and Phi Kappa Phi.

His very extensive work on British naval history made him a world authority on the subject, leading to his being invited to Oxford in 1969-70 as holder of the George Eastman visiting professorship. The inevitable resentment that British historians must have felt toward an American expert in such a field was soon extinguished by his and his wife's popularity, and he was soon rewarded with notable recognition. Oxford made him an honorary doctor of letters and the British Academy made him a corresponding Fellow.

He was awarded a special citation from the British Admiralty Board never before awarded and also the Chesney Memorial Gold Medal, presented by the Royal United Services Institution. He was the recipient of a *Festschrift* from admiring scholars from many countries, edited by a leading British historian, A. J. P. Taylor: *Naval Warfare in the Twentieth Century, 1900-1945: Essays in Honor of Arthur Marder*. The Queen made him an honorary Commander of the Order of the British Empire (C.B.E.) and Prince Philip personally commended him for his work in a field so dear to the Prince's own heart. He was a fastidiously exact scholar, a socially delightful person, and an unusually conscientious teacher.

> *A man of sharp intellect and intolerance of sham.*
> —Christopher Hill, Master of Balliol

A year or so before my official retirement from the Universitry of Southern California, I was asked to teach aboard the S.S. Universe, a floating college giving regular academic credit, on her 1974 summer voyage to the Orient. In 1975, I had a similar assignment to the Mediterranean and, in 1977, I went for a whole semester on her round-the-world voyage. These experiences evoke a panorama of nostalgic memories of many lands and many fascinating personalities. The vast variety of wonders we saw included the sacred Bo-Tree at Anuradhapura, Hindu temples at Mahabalipuram and Kanchipuram, Aurobindo's ashram at Pondicherry, the Pyramids at Cairo, King Tut's tomb in the Valley of the Kings, Ephesus, Istanbul, the Imperial Palace Museum in Taipei (where also I attended Chinese opera), the Bardo Museum near Tunis, the Roman ruins at Dougga (in the middle of nowhere, but alarmingly near the Sahara), the Alhambra, Knossos, Fez (ninth century mosque where Maimonides and Pope Sylvester II went for their studies before the European universities were even founded), and Marrakesh. It was on the second summer voyage that I first met Arthur Marder, one of the most careful and interesting scholars I have ever known and one of the kindest of men.

The ship had sailed through Panama and the Caribbean to New York where, at the dockside, my publishers had hand-delivered to me the galleys of a book of mine so that I could read them aboard and send them back corrected from Casablanca. The Marders, who had joined the ship in New York, had a nearby stateroom and we were soon exchanging civilities. At that time I knew nothing about him except that he was at the University of California at Irvine and was to be my colleague, teaching history aboard. Bewailing the prospect of a stint of proofreading on top of my teaching duties on the ship, I said half-jokingly, "I need a man of leisure to help me proofread." He replied at once with patent seriousness that he would be glad to help, adding less seriously that he happened to be the world's authority on the use and abuse of the comma. We soon became friends. He was a delightful colleague.

What a modest man he was! Sometimes he was quite boyish, despite his sixty-five years and the bald head of sagacity. He was extremely sensitive to the attitudes of those he loved and timid in making claims on their friendship. In a copy of one of his most scholarly volumes that he gave to a friend, he wrote something such as, "You may find this handy as a doorstop." Not even obliquely did he ever hint at the acclaim his work had received on both sides of the Atlantic.

Unknown to me for much of the voyage was the fact that he, an American by birth and training, was an expert on British naval history. This interest had been aroused almost by accident in his third year as a Harvard undergraduate. Professor W. L. Langer had suggested to him that, instead of the prewar German foreign policy topic that had been Marder's choice for his senior year thesis, he should consider writing on the Haldane Mission. Arthur was doubtful about this idea but decided to try his hand at it. That was how he became addicted to British naval history. From the diaries of Admiral Sir Herbert Richmond, he obtained basic pabulum for the *Portrait of an Admiral* that he published in 1952.

Arthur was indefatigable in research as in everything else to which he seriously addressed himself. His style was notably clear. He examined every shred of evidence that could be found. He was open to criticism. Above all, he learned by sheer diligence (in the etymological sense of "delighting in") to understand the ethos of the British navy.

I believe that respect for one's students is the hallmark of the best kind of teacher. Arthur Marder had it to an unusual degree. He was always trying to alleviate the ignorance of students without ever blatantly pointing it out. They appreciated this. He went further, however, treating even the youngest freshman as though he were a mature scholar. When we docked in New York on our return from the Mediterranean voyage, the pier was filled as usual on such occasions with crowds of friends and, of course, doting parents. One of the youngest students aboard was heard crying to his parents on the pier, "I took a history class from Professor Marder and he called us 'scholars and gentlemen!'" It was just what Arthur would do. He encouraged students by respecting them.

On the ship, Arthur was always on the go, but ashore he was resolutely and industriously on the run, as though there were not enough time in one's life to do all he wanted to do or hours in the day to do it with the exquisite precision he demanded of himself in all that he did. When we were on our way to, say, Malta, he would be in the ship's library poring over maps and books and by the time of our arrival he would be impatiently awaiting disembarkation. As soon as we were cleared by the immigration authorities, he was racing down the gangway and plunging into the terrain with the acuity of a Sherlock Holmes and the perseverance of a Livingstone.

In Athens, he and his charming wife, Jan, rented a car with us and we all drove to Delphi together, spending the day there and visiting the eleventh-century monastery of Hosios Lukas on the way back. He insisted on planning everything down to the last detail ahead of time and then squeezing into every moment as much of historical interest and importance as was physically possible. Now and then we teased him gently about this and he always took it amiably, usually with a fleeting but kindly smile. It made not the slightest difference to his ways, of course.

Dilatoriness was anathema to him. The patience he demanded of himself in the pursuit of his own studies and research left him with little patience for the sloth and indifference of others in the conduct of their work. The notorious unpunctuality of the Middle East sorely tried him. On one occasion, when the bus driver and local guide were twenty-five minutes late and he found his own place in the bus usurped by someone who had taken it while he was outside trying to have calls put through to get things going to schedule, he simply walked away and made private arrangements to utilize the day more profitably.

Full of admirable ideas, he would plague the administrators of the program with all sorts of proposals. He was constructively critical of every program and as intolerant of inefficiency and stupidity as he was supportive of those he admired and loved. His expectations of humanity were excessive, being based on his own unusual qualities and the demands he made on himself. A travel agent who did not know enough French even to converse with his Moroccan counterparts without being robbed right and left by them drove him to exasperation. Mistakes and muddles he found inexcusable.

Jan, his understanding and patient wife, provided the perfect complement, not to say antidote, to these qualities. With an elfin smile, she would bear his exasperations and soothe him so inconspicuously that only now and then did one notice the application of her healing balm. Yet through everything, Arthur was peculiarly endearing. He valued friendship above all else and was naturally gifted in the art without suspecting for a moment that he had any such talent, for he was in fact, as already mentioned, diffident in making even the slightest claims on a friendship. The boyishness to which I have alluded came out most endearingly in his personal relationships. It also helped to disguise the courage that was one of his noblest qualities.

He loved sartorial elegance, but nothing flashy, preferring the simplest and the best possible quality. He liked his wife to wear similarly first class quality of clothes but never showy or fussy dresses.

He was a man of truly impeccable taste, a perfect gentleman both in his outward appearance and even more in his inward disposition. Yet his reticence and modesty made both his clothes and his attitudes so inconspicuous that one hardly noticed them at the time but thought about them only in retrospect.

In contrast to parvenus who study how to show themselves off so as to get a place in the limelight, Arthur seemed to study how to avoid it.

Believing that food is as much a part of a nation's culture as is its literature or its art, he made a point of knowing not only the historical places to visit when we arrived at a port but the names and addresses of the best restaurants. He was also a collector of rare vintages of wines, which he tasted with discernment and relish.

Chinese cooking was among Arthur's hobbies. In his office was displayed with pride a diploma he had received for completing a course in it. Jan tells me that the course was given by Mary Siz in Honolulu and that Arthur actually wrote the preface to her cookbook. Yet although the ship on which we sailed together had a Mandarin-speaking Chinese captain and crew, I never suspected that hidden talent. Arthur would never have mentioned it without the strongest provocation and I never had any reason to supply this.

The last thing one would expect such a modest and reticent man to talk about would be his personal religious faith. So indeed it was. Throughout the entire voyage, I never discovered or discerned that he was Jewish by heritage or that Jan was a Christian Scientist. Still less could I have guessed that Arthur attended temple with some regularity in his years at the University of Hawaii. The nearest he ever came to the slightest hint in this direction was when, in proofreading my little book, he mentioned that he was not conversant with the subject of the book, its primary focus being a problem in the Christian doctrine of the Trinity! As with David Ritchie, the question of religion never seemed to arise in any way demanding specific attention.

Punch, in a cartoon published many decades ago, depicted the mistress of the house warning the housemaid that the new cook was a Roman Catholic, evoking the housemaid's reply that she quite understood: in the best households religion is not so much as mentioned! It was the sort of cartoon that in those days immensely tickled the British sense of humor, seeming as it did to put religion in the same category as sex.

Now that sex has become a general topic, perhaps religion will become as unmentionable in polite society as was sex in Victorian times, so vindicating the housemaid's stance. No doubt its suitability as a conversational topic depends on the company one keeps. It certainly never occurred to me to raise it with Arthur Marder and for reasons similar to those that motivated me in my relations with Ritchie. I cannot say that I felt Arthur's spirituality to be in the least like Ritchie's; nevertheless, he indubitably had a special stance of his own that did not belong to the public domain.

During his year in England, the Marders were in almost constant touch with the highest British naval dignitaries. They were many times at Blenheim Palace. High-ranking naval officers visited them almost daily and on one occasion their visitors included three admirals in one day. Arthur was everything the English seldom expect to find in an American. He must have been popular on that account alone, although no doubt it was his still more unexpected mastery of British naval history that aroused first curiosity and then admiration among the British experts.

"I look back on my Eastman year (1969-70)," wrote Arthur in *The American Oxonian* for Spring 1980, "as the richest experience of my entire academic career. The students and dons were stimulating, as was the entire way of life at Oxford." When *The Times* of London expressed wonderment that an American should have written so well on the subject of Arthur's five-volume *From the Dreadnought to Scapa Flow*, Arthur replied characteristically, "Nature abhors a vacuum and there was this fat subject waiting to be picked up." Prince Philip, however, was less astonished. In talking to Arthur on one occasion, he said that he could well see how an American scholar could write more objectively, accurately and fairly about the Royal Navy than could a British scholar standing closer to the scene.

In the last decade of his life he published *From the Dardanelles to Oran* and *Operation Menace*. The latter was a study of the attack on Dakar in 1940 and the subsequent dismissal of Admiral Sir Dudley North. Even when he knew that an inoperable cancer left him little time to work he devoted himself to a two-volume study of Anglo-Japanese naval relations from 1925 to 1945. He continued working on this project to the end.

Arthur Marder died on Christmas Day, 1980. Christopher Hill, Master of Balliol during his Oxford year, wrote of him in a letter to me after Arthur's death:

> Arthur Marder and Jan were very popular members of the Balliol community during the year when he was in Oxford as Eastman Visiting Professor and Fellow of Balliol. We all stood in some awe of his superlative scholarship, and none of us could discuss naval history with him on equal terms; but his genial kindliness and his impish sense of humour soon put us at our ease. He impressed us all as an easy, friendly, sociable member of the Common Room whom everybody liked, as well as a man of sharp intellect and intolerance of shams. He was a very great man.

ELEVEN

Catherine Wright Christie

Catherine Wright Christie (1873-1959) was born five minutes after midnight on May 18, 1873, in Dundee, Scotland, where also she died at half past four in the afternoon of January 25, 1959. The whole of her professional life was spent as a kindergarten teacher, although when the following account opens, in August of 1914, that Germanic term had gone speedily out of fashion with the outbreak of World War I. At that time, women were still disfranchised. Despite the vigorous campaigns of the suffragettes, voting rights in Britain were not to be granted till 1918 and then, at first, only to women over thirty. Moreover, because of the prevailing industries in Dundee, there was an extreme imbalance between the male and female populations so that, with a vast preponderance of women over men, a girl's opportunities for marriage were, to say the least, slender. For a young woman of some little education and a way with children, elementary school teaching offered a dignity and security that in such circumstances brought her some degree of envy but always considerable respect, irrespective of the social stratum to which she belonged in those class-ridden days.

Miss Christie, at the time to which the following account relates, was in her early forties, although to the very small children entrusted to her care, she seemed venerably old. Having been already teaching children of kindergarten age for some twenty years, she was, however, thoroughly experienced. She was not only a mistress of her craft; she had a natural wisdom and insight and a love for her charges that was by no means universal in an age when her profession too often tended to turn disgruntled spinsters into sadistic perverts. Miss Christie, however, whose entire life was spent obscurely in narrow circumstances, seemed always to exude kindliness and to inspire a sense of that fairness we all love and too seldom find in human life.

She drew out of me what I somehow already knew and wanted so much to retrieve, much as the slave in Plato's Meno *remembered geometry from a previous existence.*

I was escorted to kindergarten at the age of four, two weeks after the declaration, on August 4, 1914, that Britain was at war with Germany: the outbreak of World War I. An only child, I had been nurtured in an atmosphere of love but (being of elderly parentage, with a maternal grandmother born in 1828 and still very much flourishing) I had few playmates of my own age. Even my acquaintance with older people had been largely limited to my parents' circle of friends. Going to school was, therefore, a more than ordinarily exciting and fearsome adventure.

I was somewhat precocious, having learned the alphabet at three and being by then able to read words and even some short poems and simple stories. My grandmother had started a literacy campaign upon me at the age of two, teaching me new words to which she always automatically added the spelling—for example, "That is ivy, eye-vee-wye." The notion that words are written and read as well as spoken and heard was impressed upon me even before I had mastered the alphabet.

Some weeks before I went to school, I had heard people say that "the war clouds are gathering." It had been a dark day with black clouds on the horizon and I supposed that this was a prelude to a state of affairs that was generally accounted evil. By this time I could read the word "war" in the newspaper headlines. I asked many questions about it. The answers I received were by no means reassuring. I could also read the word "front" and learned that it was the place where war was waged. Soon I was launched into my own battlefield.

As my mother led me in midmorning to take my place in the class that had already begun the day's work, every member of the class rose, folding the little benches behind each desk as noiselessly as inexpert tiny hands could contrive and then stood stiffly to attention. Miss Christie surveyed the class to check that the rite of standing to attention had been duly performed. She then uttered a further order, which sounded to me "Standardese," filling me with apprehension that I might not be able to cope with the vocabulary of the society into which I was being thrust, for I had no idea what it could mean. She then greeted my mother, who smiled back of course. They exchanged a very few words, after which, with a wistful smile in my direction, she delivered me into the hands of the teacher, whom she addressed as

"Miss Christie." Her given name was not known to me and would have seemed as private a matter as the color of her petticoat.

Miss Christie looked benign enough in her way and I was well accustomed to dealing with people of her age. She had dark hair, clear blue eyes; her face was long in shape, her complexion ruddy, and her features sharp. As I surveyed her from her black boots that peeked out under her long black skirt and white blouse, all the way up to her not unfriendly face, I could see nothing objectionable. Still, my fears were not entirely allayed, for, to prepare me for the worst, I had been warned that school was a hard place, where teachers kept children in order with the aid of a painful instrument—a strap or cane.

My eyes wandered momentarily toward the class, for I had been also warned of the cruelties that children perpetrate on the weak and defenseless and especially on those who do not conform to tribal custom. The class contained two sections, the boys on the left (from the teacher's standpoint) and the girls on the right. As I scanned their little faces, I could detect neither friendliness nor hostility. I felt the excitement of adventure. At last the day had come, the day I had for so long heard about. I was entering upon a new world, plunging into the unknown. The impact of the experience was overwhelming and enduring. It was perhaps in some unconscious way connected in my mind with the experience of birth itself.

Miss Christie, pointing to an empty place in the third row from the front of the boys' section, enjoined me to go thither. I did so, standing like a half-shut knife, for I had not yet learned how to prize the seat back to enable me to stand up straight as the others had done. Miss Christie, having bidden her adieu to my mother, then announced my name to the class and informed me that the boy immediately to my left, who shared the double desk with me, bore the name of Willie Soutar.

She then gave the order "Attention!" whereupon the company of male and female miniature pseudosoldiers snapped back stiffly into poker-like immobility. I did as best I could, no doubt even more clumsily than the rest. We then received the order to sit, at which Willie, who like most of the class was nearly a year older than I, prodded me in the shin under the desk and grinned sideways in my direction.

Miss Christie's eagle eye fell instantly upon him and her voice, no longer gentle, rasped out, "Willie! Eyes *front!*" Five-year-old Willie resumed his studious demeanor, for well had he detected that, as she spoke, she had glanced ever so slightly toward the drawer wherein he knew was kept the dreaded instrument of pain. Instinctively, I knew that must be the place where it lay all ready for the punishment of wickedness and vice, to say nothing of the maintenance of true religion and virtue.

As Miss Christie entered the aisle and bore down upon me, my heart leapt into my mouth. I can still hear it pounding. I dared not even look to see whether the face high above me bore the signs of kindness or anger. I feared too much that she was about to descend upon me to bring me by the collar to the floor, the place of wrath, for some infraction I might have unwittingly committed or perhaps just on general principles, by way of introducing a neophyte to the terrors of the new life on which he was embarking. To my intense delight, she merely said in a quiet, matter-of-fact tone, "Just copy what Willie is doing."

Willie, I quickly discovered, was simply making vertical strokes on the bottom half of his slate, which I took to be inexpert attempts at the letter *I*. On top he had made a series of crosses, which I took to be similarly crude attempts at the letter *X*. My theory, not an unreasonable one, was exploded a moment or two later by Miss Christie's reminder to the class that we were making a representation of a field of corn (the generic name we gave to any kind of growing grain: oats, wheat, or whatever) on a starry night. Obediently, I copied Willie's efforts. Nevertheless, I recall my distinct feeling of disappointment. I had feared that my literary talents should not measure up to the demands of school, the new world on which I had entered, and here we were engaged in what seemed to me childish exercises far below the level of my attainment.

When however, a little later in the morning, I saw the teacher write a few letters on the blackboard, I cheered up. I noticed they were all capitals.

"What is this letter?" she inquired of a pudding-faced boy who jumped to attention and yelled "A." By the time she came to *D*, she had to call for volunteers and, when she had reached *E*, they were few. I was too timid to raise my hand. She then asked the class if anyone among us knew how many letters there are. Not a hand was raised.

Suddenly, no doubt to accustom me to speaking in class, even if only to say I did not know, she asked *me* whether, perhaps, *I* knew. I replied in a quiet voice, for I was then extremely shy, "Twenty-six," which up till then I had accounted a truism not fit to be uttered aloud. She returned me a quick, half-astonished look, immediately hidden. Thereupon, in a moment of inspiration, exhilaration, or *je-ne-sais-quoi*, I recited the entire alphabet at breakneck speed, concluding with the accepted British usage of the day, "zed and dot."[1]

Miss Christie, never batting an eye, merely nodded and proceeded to discuss the next letter, *F*, which she described as an *E* with the bottom ledge missing. She wished the class to repeat it till she told us to stop. Over and over again came the repetitive chanted replies through thirty sets of baby teeth.

On went the lesson till the bell rang loud and mightily and the class waited eagerly for Miss Christie's almighty word of permission to stand, the command to snap to attention, and eventually, the order to leave, which was done in single file, aisle by aisle, girls first, doubling as we reached the door and then proceeding in double rows under the surveillance of sharp-eyed teachers in the corridors, until we had separated into two outdoor areas of anarchy, male and female, respectively. Miss Christie, however, had signalled me to remain while the others left.

"Can you read *words*?" she asked. I felt the eager curiosity in her voice.

"Yes," I replied very simply and in a tone such as most of us would use in reply to the question, "Have you ten toes?"

Sphinx-like, she continued, "Could you read this?"

I looked at the thin paperback book she offered me. It happened to be one I knew well. It was open, moreover, at the page on which was a picture of a cow and underneath it, one of my favorite poems.

"What is it?"

"It is a cow, see-oh-double-you," I replied nonchalantly. Then, seeing her finger guiding me to the first word I went on, reading in my childish singsong and at top speed:

The cow, the friendly cow, all red and white
I love with all my heart;
She gives me milk with all her might
To eat with apple tart.

Then I looked up with my then soft brown eyes into her earnest blue ones. She was staring at me, but the stare lasted only a split second after she caught mine. She turned to another page, covered the writing with her hand, and inquired the name of the animal depicted.

I hesitated only an instant, then replied, "I think it is a lion, ell-eye-oh-enn," I ventured. Then as she withdrew her hand and exposed the writing, I said, "Oh no, it is a tiger, tee-eye-gee-ee-ar." I had never thought of dissociating the spelling from the word. Moreover, as the reader will have noticed, my zoological knowledge was somewhat behind my literary prowess.

Never shall I forget the look in her eyes as I raised mine again to hers. In them, I perceived a tenderness and love I had never before seen outside my own family circle, where it was a regular part of the scenery. They seemed milky moist and for a moment, she looked at me as though she were about to embrace me, which, however, I instinctively knew to be unthinkable in the teaching relationship. Her voice remained brisk as she cleared her throat and went on, "You read well. You have been well taught. Your father?"

"No."

"Your mother?"

"No. Myself."

A vestige of a smile passed over her lips. Her incredulity was not, however, so entirely justified as she thought, for although, of course, I had received the tools and some help, I had, in fact, been so eager to learn the alphabet that I really had done much of the learning on my own; nor had that seemed to me in the least unusual. After all, I had had no means of making a comparative analysis.

"You will be ahead of the others for some time," she remarked. In her voice was an exaggeratedly matter-of-fact intonation. "See that they don't catch up with you. Meanwhile, you will have to go over the alphabet with the others till they learn it. It will do you no harm."

Her words, "It will do you no harm," lingered long in my ears. Wasn't it going to be a bit dull? Of course, I had no choice and I knew it. What I did not know, unless in some unconscious cavern of my mind, was that I had made an instant conquest, doomed to the awful fate of being soon destined to be marked with the hateful and opprobrious label I was to come to dread like the stigma of a felon: "Teacher's Pet." I do not think I was ever actively hated in kindergarten, but now and then I felt the resentment of some members of our infantile society. Almost daily I was in fear of hearing the sting of the epithet. Miss Christie, however, was a willing partner in my efforts to give no grounds for the charge, although it would not have been easy for either of us to deny its justice.

When I returned from my first day of kindergarten (which, by the way, we unashamedly called "baby school," since the former, being German, had gone out of fashion at once), my grandmother happened to be in the house. I began to recount my adventures but as my triumphs were unfolded, she merely went on nodding a repetitive "of course." I told her with great solemnity that Miss Christie, who had become in my eyes a close runnerup to God, had warned me not to fall behind the others.

My grandmother, who obviously judged that to be an unthinkable calamity, replied that I could begin by learning a new word there and then. So far, all the words I knew were monosyllabic or nearly so, but why should I not try a more interesting word? She admitted that it would be difficult, but then life is full of difficulties so it would be good to dispose of one of them right away. The word was "supercilious."

"What does it mean?" I asked.

Rising to her full height of about five feet, she raised her eyebrows and stared down at my feet with a look of utter contempt.

"That," she informed me, "is looking supercilious."

I laughed and tried to copy her and she laughed a little too, but proceeded with the business. I had so much trouble with the new word that she was forced to cut it in half. I would learn the first half today and the next half tomorrow. So I learned 'super ess-yoo-pee-ee-ar," the first of many words more difficult than I had ever learned before. Occasionally, I would spring one on my new goddess, Miss Christie.

Next morning, just after the door had been closed, Miss Christie led the class in the customary prayer (we were judged too young for the Lord's Prayer) which was, "Dear God, bless our teacher and bless us. Guide us and guard us wherever we go. Amen." Since I had long been taught to use a similar one every day by my bedside on waking, no sense of liturgical novelty troubled me and I duly sat down with the rest of the class at the conclusion of this simple prayer, to which, surely, no adherent of any of the great religions of the world could have taken grave exception on theological or other grounds.

I was eagerly awaiting the continuation of our literary studies when the door opened. A very forlorn-looking little boy appeared and murmured an apparently lameduck excuse to Miss Christie, whose face was becoming sterner with every word. A little girl in the front row seemed to have heard the excuse and giggled. She was promptly summoned to the floor to join her partner in crime.

Without ado, Miss Christie opened the drawer of the desk and took out the instrument of pain, the tawse—a long, black, narrow, two-thong strap. I gulped at the sight of it. (Could I have seen then the larger and much heavier straps that as older boys we were destined to behold in daily use, I might have fainted at the sight.) When the boy had extended his tiny palm, Miss Christie administered one quick, efficient overhead swipe and the boy returned to his seat sobbing. The little girl then received a milder whack and returned likewise weeping and with the warning that if she giggled anymore she would be thrashed "hard, like a boy." That was my first introduction to sex discrimination. Had we boys thought it out we should probably have been strongly in favor of women's liberation. Since my mother was a suffragette, I had already some inkling of the nature of the issue. My concern, however, at that moment, was with what I should do if I were called upon to be the recipient of the same treatment. Could I bear the pain? Perhaps even more fearsome to contemplate: would Miss Christie let me off, so exposing me to the vengeance of the class, their ridicule, and no doubt their physical abuse? I was not sure which would be the more terrible fate.

I was spared both of these anxieties (as well as the boredom of following the elementary linguistic studies of the class) by the comparatively primitive medical knowledge of the day. Two weeks after my triumphant entry upon my new world, I was stricken by measles. Presumably, I must have caught them almost the first morning. Staying in bed day after day was a new experience that distracted me a little from thoughts of school. Then I was back in school for only another week or two when once again I was laid low, this time with whooping cough. Within the two years that constituted baby school, I had almost every one of the "diseases of children" except diphtheria, which was common and much feared. The worst for me was scarlet fever, from which I almost died. I remember the doctor taking a perfunctory look at my back and groaning as he saw the rash.

That time, however, I was greatly perturbed, because Miss Christie had promised that she would tell us a wonderful story. In my delirium, I recited poems I had learned and recounted stories that Miss Christie had told us. In trying to retell one of her stories, I stuck at the same place over and over again and became so hysterical at my inability to go on, that an emissary was sent to Miss Christie's home in the evening to ask for the information. Miss Christie, who, of couse, could not dare to visit a scarlet fever patient, wrote the whole story out in her own hand. When it was brought home, it was read to me and I was much consoled, but the fever was reaching its worst and that night I was alternately conscious and delirious.

That was the night they feared I might die. I remember my grandmother telling me that Miss Christie was praying for me, as well as my parents and aunts, and that she herself would remain at my side praying that my life be spared. Every time I regained consciousness, I was aware of her praying softly by my side. Eventually, I fell asleep for what seemed a lifetime.

The delirium must have passed and the fever must have gone down, for when I awoke, I clearly saw her rising from her knees. As she went to the window to open the curtains, the sun (a wintry one) was already shining and I could see how tired she was. Nor was that remarkable; she was then eighty-seven. Yet her face shone with the triumph of one who had wrestled with the Lord and won. She said very quietly, "God has answered all our prayers. He has spared your life."

She then fell on her knees by my bed and, enjoining me to lie very still, she thanked God in a torrent of grateful prayers, asking his blessing on all who had joined in the prayers, including Miss Christie. I could see she was weeping, which was something I had never seen an adult do. I could not have understood that, mingled with her emotions, was no doubt the remembrance that she had been one of ten children, all of whom except herself had died in infancy during the reign of George IV. She told me a little later on that, when I was better, I must write to thank Miss Christie—a very beautiful letter to her, because she had no children of her own.

Miss Christie remained my idol throughout baby school, which consisted of two years divided into four "steps" that were in fact semesters. On one occasion, a little girl in the class died. Boys and girls were so effectively segregated, despite our coeducational instruction, that we boys hardly knew the girls at all and had no idea what really went on in their heads. Miss Christie suggested to us, however, that we should all, boys and girls, make a small contribution to buy a floral wreath and that she would choose a few of us to accompany her after school, on the eve of the funeral, to make the selection. It was my first experience of quasidemocratic procedure and I must say it struck me as very odd, for at that time, my political sense was almost nil. We were shown three or four bell glasses with wax flowers and pretty birds under them. Without much controversy, to say the least, we accepted Miss Christie's choice and adjourned with a sense of satisfaction that an important ritual had been performed.

Later, I asked Miss Christie why the little girl had died. Instead of giving the medical reason, which most teachers would have been content to give, she told me that some people die after a long life, others after a short one, because God has tasks for all of us and some tasks take longer than do others. Her answer puzzled me a little, but I put great trust in Miss Christie's wisdom. The more I thought about her answer, the more sense it seemed to make.

Despite the segregation of boys and girls, even at that early age (except in class where we sat in different parts of the same room) and despite the fact that there was a sort of unwritten taboo even among ourselves against talking to the girls, such converse very occasionally occurred. One day after school, a girl in the class overtook me and engaged me in conversation. She was a jovial, rosy-faced, buxsom little girl bearing the name of May Moncrieffe, and I had to confess to myself that I found her very pleasant. I wished we might meet often and play together. I was five at the time and the lady of this daring adventure probably six. News of our encounter and fifty-yard walk together spread like wildfire. Even my elders at home teased me affectionately about it. Mercifully, Miss Christie said nothing; but I felt so embarrassed that I never dared to talk to my little ladyfriend again.

We boys, at that age, sedulously cultivated the opinion that girls were an utterly alien breed. I fully subscribed to the general opinion that their existence was inexplicable. They were there because they were there. They wore strange, fluffy, frilly clothes and giggled almost

constantly, sometimes even in school, if they could get away with it.
Their ways were so different from ours that it rarely occurred to us
that they might make good companions. So my romance was nipped in
the bud. Had Miss Christie mentioned it, I wonder how I could have
withstood the embarrassment. The way some other people went on,
one might have thought we had committed adultery.

One day, near the end of my time under Miss Christie's tutelage,
Miss Christie suddenly collapsed. She simply slid down on her chair
and onto the floor where she lay motionless on her back. Her
"pointer," a long wooden one, with which she had been calling to our
attention the figures on the blackboard, crashed down on the floor
beside her. The class gasped. Some of us, in consternation, looked at
one another, wondering what we ought to do. At last, we somehow
decided that we must go out and find another teacher and tell her what
had happened. By the time we had returned with the other teacher,
however, Miss Christie had recovered and was sitting in her chair,
which she seldom used, for she generally taught standing and she
walked a great deal up and down the aisles among us. When the other
teacher had departed, Miss Christie spoke in a low voice to the hushed
class.

"You will have to be very, very good today, because I am not well."
Then she asked a boy to retrieve her pointer. This done, she resumed
the arithmetic lesson while seated. The class was exceptionally well
behaved for the rest of the day. I remember wishing I could have done
something special to help Miss Christie and thinking how terrible it
would be if she were too ill to come back. What if she were no longer
our teacher? For the first time, I could see the bottom falling out of my
world. Nor were my fears unjustified, for as we shall soon see I was
about to be catapulted into a world so different that it seemed almost
like another life.

My deep love for Miss Christie was sanctified by the respect in
which my family held her. My own respect for her was boundless.
Whenever I had the slightest difficulty with schoolwork, she would
explain to me very clearly and simply where the difficulty lay.

Occasionally, a visiting teacher, usually very young, would be
imported for a morning or so. I was very conscious of her inexperience
and other shortcomings. Yet I never really compared such young
hopefuls to Miss Christie, who was not only mistress of all she taught
(which included a great deal of useful information far beyond the rigid
kindergarten curriculum) but had also a profound insight into the
workings of my mind. The youth, vigor, and enthusiasm of the young
women who appeared now and then in the classroom did not in the
least impress me, nor did my qualities affect them. One of them

punished me severely for no apparent reason at all. So well behaved was I in baby school that only twice in the two years did Miss Christie punish me, both time for a minor infractions, and so gently that it hardly hurt at all physically, although displeasing her caused me great internal remorse. I bore not the slightest resentment on either occasion, knowing how embarrassing would have been any attempt to overlook my crimes, not least since, in those days, many of the boys and some of the girls were punished almost every other day.

My first two years at school had been made idyllic by Miss Christie's intelligence and compassion, making me feel assured that the world outside could be almost as loving as the one I knew at home. The *Aufklärung* quickly came. My next few years were governed by a series of female sadists, succeeded, when I was about eleven, by a team of male sadists.

When I was eight, for instance, we suffered under a singularly cruel, uncomely spinster who not only administered the tawse (hers a particularly painful one) for the most trivial offenses, but sometimes added a punishment of her own devising—that by which an offender was "kept in" during the midmorning break. The cruelty of this device lay in the fact that by that age we were thoroughly indoctrinated with the belief that we ought to be able to control our needs during school hours and that, being no longer babies, the idea of our asking permission to leave the room was out of the question. Morning classes ran for three and a half hours and the ten-minute break was the only opportunity afforded for the relief of distended bladders. Denial of that opportunity usually entailed grievous pain and distress coupled with fear of the unthinkable humiliation that even a momentary lapse of fortitude could bring. All this, we firmly believed (no doubt with reason) was inflicted with the calculated intent of producing such consequences. We unaffectionately called our tormentor "The Bear."

Then, for some time when I was about nine, we had an elderly male alcoholic who spent half the day gibbering to himself. At twelve, one of my schoolmasters was a casebook sadist who openly leered as he delightedly administered the tawse and mocked those who could not, as the unwritten law required, hide the agony his savage beatings inflicted. I understand that, many years after I had left school, he was escorted from the classroom to a mental institution.

Miss Christie, by contrast, had forever captured the heart and trained the mind of a somewhat precocious and very imaginative child. She encouraged the development of imagination within a framework of the most rigorous drill in what were accounted the essentials of an elementary education. She seemed to belong to another age as to some extent, of course, she did.

I felt as though we had known each other from time immemorial and that she was somehow part of my total destiny. She did not openly shower love upon me as did the bevy of elderly female relatives I knew, at the center of which, of course, was my mother; but somehow I knew that Miss Christie was my appointed guide into a world whither others could not go to guide me. My gratitude to her was and has remained infinite. Yet I never learned much about her that biographers would account fundamental. There seemed no need to know. What she did for me, in her distant, quiet way, seems far too important for such trivial information to matter.

I do not think anyone ever again taught me so much so easily and in so short a time till (it seems a trillion lifetimes later) Austin Farrer did the same for me at, of course, a different level. Yet Miss Christies's level was the most fundamental of all. And she did not so much teach me as draw out of me what I somehow already knew and wanted so much to retrieve, much as the slave in Plato's *Meno* remembered geometry from a previous existence.

Catherine W. Christie

Catherine Wright Christie

TWELVE

A Miscellany of Acquaintances

I remarked in the preface that when I tell young people today that, in my youth, I met G. K. Chesterton and Rudyard Kipling, I might almost as well say Shakespeare and Milton. For the former no less than the latter were dead long before these young people were born. In my youth, however, although I revered such distinguished men, meeting them did not seem particularly remarkable. Otherwise, I should probably have tried to see much more of them. As things are, however, they are among those whom I met only briefly or occasionally and who are, therefore, included in this miscellany.

I met Chesterton at Claridge's, London, at a luncheon given by the Royal Society of Literature on July 12, 1933. He was very portly indeed and his girth, together with the gold chain on his waistcoat, the old-fashioned moustache, and the still more old-fashioned pince-nez, gave him a somewhat mayoral appearance. For in those days, at any rate, portliness (the result of excessive banqueting) was an occupational hazard of high civic office and was often accompanied by a slightly outmoded style of manner and dress. Chesterton enjoyed poking fun at his own corpulence. Having been called upon to speak immediately after Kipling, he naturally paid tribute to the latter's celebrity. By that time, more than a quarter of a century had passed since Kipling had received the Nobel Prize for Literature. His name was a household word in every educated home in the British Empire.

Chesterton suggested that we must all be puzzled at his occupying any space, let alone so large a space, in such a distinguished assembly. He went on to say, however, to the astonishment of us all, that despite Mr. Kipling's celebrated literary talents, he could outdo him on one score. Chesterton claimed that his superiority was in the realm of politeness. The audience held their breath, awaiting an explanation of this outrageously unbecoming claim. He was, he persisted the politest man in all England.

"I am the only man in England," he went on, "who can get up in a bus and offer his place to *three* ladies."

Since the occasion was a welcoming of the Canadian Authors' Association, he alluded to his having visited Canada on two occasions. He said the Canadians were so hospitable that they rushed out into the street to meet and greet him and he, having been taken to be a literary man (as a result of the general confusion), had to keep up the pretense. He added that he intended to continue to do so during the present luncheon. He noted that, in his day, he had said almost as much in making fun of the British Empire as Mr. Kipling had said in praise of it; nevertheless, he much appreciated the liberty Canadians had provided to people escaping from American tyrannies across the border, first from slavery and then from prohibition, which he hinted was an even more oppressive state of society. I had already developed a lively admiration for Chesterton's work and was delighted to hear him deliver such an amusing speech.

Chesterton's use of paradox in his Catholic polemic against the nineteenth-century agnosticism he had formerly espoused was, if not always universally convincing, usually refreshing. A considerable essayist, novelist, and critic, he was also the author of some remarkable poems and at times could rival Swift as a satirist. His poem entitled *Antichrist*, for instance, may well be the most mordant satire in the English language on the subject of religious hypocrisy. It was inspired by a remark made by F. E. Smith, the future Lord Birkenhead, who was, in his day, probably the most brilliant legal counsel in the Empire. Smith, briefed to oppose a bill that was before Parliament for the disestablishment of the Welsh Church, had called it "a bill which has shocked the conscience of every Christian community in Europe." This, although fairly normal political boilerplate and no doubt delivered with much razzle-dazzle, was too much for Chesterton, who was moved in his poem to inquire whether Breton sailors and Russian peasants in mountain hamlets were distressed at the possibility of the disestablishment of the Church of Wales and whether Christians in the Middle East were less grieved at their friends being killed by Muslims, now that a curate lived in Cardiff, thanks to the work of F. E. Smith. He concluded by urging Smith to talk as much as he pleased about pews and steeples and the emoluments of ecclesiastical office but to shut up about the souls of Christian peoples.[1]

Among the more literary, less liturgical hymns that have won a permanent place in English hymnody, Chesterton's "O God of earth and altar" is still impressive, much more so, for instance, than Kipling's "God of our fathers, known of old," while nowhere in English literature is there a neater or more startling dramatization of the saga

of England than in his poem *The Secret People.*
Trevelyan, reflecting on the results of Henry V's campaigns asks, "What had we gained by the long, persistent endeavour to erect an English Empire in Europe?" And he answers, "We had most justly earned the break-up of our own medieval society and a period of anarchy and moral prostration. We gained the port of Calais which we kept for another hundred years . . . ."[2] Chesterton, in a robust lyrical kaleidoscope, describes in a few magnificent stanzas the whole history of England in such a way as to show England as an island fortress filled with lovable, laughing people, content with their lot yet misunderstood by all other nations because they "have not spoken yet."[3] Even at the side of so famous a figure as Kipling, Gilbert Keith Chesterton was a truly great man—visionary and poet, satirist and prophet—whose flair for paradox as a literary device concealed for some the profundity of his thought.

I had the privilege of seeing Albert Schweitzer in 1931, when he received two honorary degrees, one in divinity, the other in music, at the same graduation ceremony at the University of Edinburgh. I recall how unaffected he was, carrying his Leonardesque mind and deep religious insight and wisdom with an air of rustic simplicity. He was enthusiastically cheered, of course, for already by that time, he was internationally famed among New Testament scholars for his work on the quest for the historical Jesus, as well as known to a much wider public for his medical missionary work at Lambaréné. Perhaps fewer at that time fully appreciated the implications of his philosophical principle of "reverence for life." I certainly wish I could then have more adequately understood it. In the context of evolutionism, it is perhaps the most deeply religious concept in twentieth-century Christian thought.

I met Charles Williams at Oxford in the mid-forties in the rooms of a friend at St. John's who had invited me for the occasion. Williams, talking on his favorite theme, the Grail, spoke with undonnish passion and zest. He had a distinctly elfin quality. The room was not nearly commodious enough for the audience and became so stuffy that we had to have an intermission so that we could all go outside and imbibe some fresh air. He returned to the fray with more nervous energy than ever to continue his torrents of eloquence.

About the same time, I met C.S. Lewis, whose conversion from donnish skepticism to a fairly orthodox Christian stance had astonished his Oxford colleagues and stirred many all over the English-speaking world. Having just read *The Screwtape Letters,* I somehow expected him to be a thin, wiry, perhaps feisty don. Instead, I found a man in his forties, more like a jovial monk or farmer than an English literature don. His voice was pleasantly fullthroated. Although definite in the expression of his opinions, his tone in discussion was conciliatory. I met him several times and came to know him moderately well in a casual way.

Very different was the personality of another Christian Oxonian of the period, Dorothy L. Sayers, whom I encountered only once. She spoke that evening neither on her detective fiction nor on her religious writings. Her topic was "The English People." It was held in a room in one of the men's colleges—Balliol, perhaps. She was dressed very tweedily and came on strong, with a fearsome array of forcefully nationalistic dogmas. Her subject, she insisted, was Englishness, which excluded therefore the interests of any Scots, Welsh, or Irish who might be in her audience. She certainly adhered with fidelity to her subject and said some interesting things about it, although she gave me the impression at the time of being ready to punch in the nose anyone who might be harboring audacious thoughts of disagreeing with anything she might say. One point she made has remained in my mind: English national feeling is at its maximum not in conservative Yorkshire or old-fashioned Devon, but on the south coast, where awareness of "us" and "them" has always been strongest. To my disappointment, she never alluded even in passing to anything pertaining to the Christian faith, on which she had written so interestingly; nor did she say anything about her special form of craftsmanship in the writing of detective stories.

I never met W.R. Inge, the farfamed dean of St. Paul's Cathedral, London, but, in my early twenties, I heard him preach from his own pulpit. At a much later time, he wrote a favorable review of my first book for *The British Weekly*. In the course of the review, however, he opined that its author was apparently a somewhat extreme Anglo-Catholic. The reviewer in *The Times Literary Supplement* seems to have had a similar opinion. I may indeed have seemed so, but I was in fact a Scottish Presbyterian both by family tradition and, at the time, ecclesiastical allegiance. My inclinations were, in fact, much closer to the tradition of Christian Platonism in which he himself stood than to any kind of Church partisanship, all forms of which have always bored me as tending to minister to non-think. However, from my earliest teens, when I first took an interest in religion, I have always felt more at home in a Catholic ambience than in a Protestant one.

During a semester at Heidelberg University in 1938, just before Neville Chamberlain went on his illstarred diplomatic mission to

Munich, I met and attended the lectures of various German scholars, including those of Martin Dibelius. At that time, Hitler was at the zenith of his power, shortly after the *Anschluss*. When I had crossed into Austria a few weeks after it had been absorbed into the German hegemony, I ate lunch at a little country inn. On my departing, the two daughters of the family curtsied in the lovely old-fashioned way, saying *"Grüss Gott,"* the traditional greeting in Austria and Bavaria. Their mother, taking no chances with a stranger, rushed out to rebuke them pointedly in my presence. *"Ihr sollt dass nicht sagen. Ihr sollt 'Heil Hitler' sagen.'*[2]

University professors followed the same principle, greeting their classes with hand upraised in the ancient Roman manner with the greeting "Heil Hitler." Dibelius was the only one in my experience who never did so, going straight into his subject as soon as he entered the classroom. His lectures were models of careful organization and his diction so clear that even with limited German I had acquired on my own shortly before going to Heidelberg, I could understand a good deal. Like most German professors, he was very formal in class, although he could be friendly and even warm in private, in a reserved sort of way.

In Paris just after the war, I happened to attend High Mass one Sunday at Notre Dame. When most of the congregation had left the great cathedral, I struck up a conversation with a middle-aged priest who, like myself, had dallied. Having noticed a peculiarity in the liturgical behavior of the people, I inquired about it only to receive the customary Gallic shrug and the response, "Ah, une mauvaise habitude, c'est tout!" (Oh, just a bad habit, that's all!) We continued to talk, however, and it turned out that he was a Trappist, which somewhat surprised me, since one does not expect members of that extremely enclosed and notoriously strict Order to be galavanting in metropolitan areas such as Paris. He was especially interested in what I could tell him of the new Trappist house at Nunraw in the Scottish Lothians, the first Cistercian house in Scotland since the Reformation. Then, if only to keep the conversation going, I asked if the mother house of the order, the Grande Trappe, still functioned. He smiled gently. He was a relaxed man with a pleasant, open face above the long black coat that all but covered his white habit. Loosening his coat a little, he revealed the pectoral cross as he told me he was the Abbot of the Grande Trappe and would be very pleased to receive me there as a guest any time I felt inclined to visit the abbey.

Eventually, I did, leaving with the nine o'clock electric train from the Gare Montparnasse to Laigle and thence to Soligny by bus, as he had recommended. He had not mentioned a five- or six-kilometer walk from Soligny to the abbey, at which I arrived at nearly two in the afternoon. It is a dull building in early nineteenth-century mock-Gothic (almost all the original structures were demolished during the French Revolution); yet a visit there teaches one more about the Middle Ages than ever could be learned at Chartres or the Sainte Chapelle. Even a week on Mount Athos in 1964 gave me hardly any better sense of the medieval way of life.

Having tugged the bellpull at the main gateway, I heard a clanking sound inside, then saw in the doorway as it slowly opened, the figure of a lay brother clad in coarse brown cloth. Bearded, slightly bent, with one good eye and for the other a blind socket, he looked as if straight out of Victor Hugo. A moment later, I found him talking as if from another century.

Soon we were together on the cobbled stone of the courtyard, with the door secured against the world. He was walking up and down muttering to himself about "Our Very Reverend Father Abbot" (*notre très révérend Père Abbé*) and obviously perplexed to know just what to do with the strange being from outside who claimed that the abbot was expecting him. At last, he suggested that it would be best for me to meet the guest master first. The latter duly appeared, a young priest with a translucent pink and white face above his yellowish-white woolen habit. He spoke very slowly and in studied English, "Is it zat you speak French?"

I said I did and he replied that it would be easier for him. He then asked when I had last eaten and I confessed that it had been seven hours ago and I should be glad of a little sustenance.

"It will be better if you eat first. Then I shall take you to *notre très révérend Père Abbé.* In a little room across another courtyard, I found myself seated in front of a French omelette. The guest master remained standing in silence by my side.

"No, thank you. We stand in the presence of a guest," he explained in answer to my protest. "Humility, you understand."

I thought of the story of the Trappist novice who, when asked to enumerate the virtues of the various orders, replied, "For missionary enterprise the Jesuits, of course; for liturgy the Benedictines; for Holy Poverty the Franciscans; but for humility we Trappists beat the whole damn lot."

Eventually, I was escorted up the rather impressive staircase and into the presence of the Abbot, who received me in a very matter-of-fact way. We talked about my occupation, which I described as "teaching philosophy."

"*Ah, oui, la philosophie,*" he mused. "Today it is existentialism; tomorrow it will be something else; *mais nous avons la vérité.*" We have the truth! He said it as one might say, "We have the Crown Jewels, all securely locked up in the vault." He was a serene man, obviously dedicated to the administration of his historic abbey. He said he would like to show me over the monastery, but for two reasons he was going to ask his righthand man, the Prior, to do so. First, he had some urgent work he must do; second, the Prior, although French, had been to school at Stonyhurst and would like the opportunity to speak English, an art that he, the Abbot, had never acquired.

Lifting the receiver of an antique telephone, he announced himself, "Dominus." He said the last syllable with a French u and the first with the bell-like o of the French donnez. This signal from the Abbot automatically granted permission to speak, apart from which no monk might ever speak except in emergencies such as fire or flood, and when necessary to direct the day's work. ("Today I am to plow this field, you that one.") Otherwise, communication had to be by sign language.

The Prior came in, still loosening the leather thongs that had hoisted his habit to facilitate some agricultural chore in which he had been engaged when summoned to the abbatial presence. The monastery, at that time, had only seventy-five monks. A full complement to run the establishment would have been more like double that number, so they were very shorthanded. When, as we crossed the fields, I noticed a brand new American tractor, I expressed some surprise at such modernity. The Prior explained how important it was to use all modern devices they could get. It helped them to be as self-sufficient as possible. As things were, they had to go to the village to buy certain items and that minimal contact with the world was not as they would wish.

He was taking me, he said, to the barns. That was where they slept during the war. He explained that when the Germans had occupied that part of Normandy in May 1940, they had demanded the use of the abbey. They wanted it for a hospital.

He then told of a more astonishing circumstance. Although the war had been in progress for eight or nine months and the Abbot knew this, he had not deemed it necessary to tell the other monks, not even the Prior. With the Germans on their doorstep, however, he had decided to call a chapter and explain that a war was going on and some adjustments would have to be made in their life.

"You slept in the barns for the duration of the war?" I asked. "That must have been very hard."

He looked at me, puzzled. "Hard?" He translated aloud to himself, "Dur ?" Then he smiled broadly and said, "I think we shall now go to see the dormitory."

That explained his initial incomprehension. The monks had much enjoyed the luxury of sleeping on straw. Normally, they sleep on narrow boards, fully clothed in their habits, with only a little panel of wood between their heads to prevent them from breathing on each other. They rise at one-thirty in the morning, after six hours' sleep. He showed me the bathing arrangements: a portable zinc bath, passed down the line of monks out of which each man gives himself a quick rubdown. The water is always cold; in winter, it must be almost freezing. I had not the temerity to inquire whether humility dictated the order of ablutions—the most junior novice getting the clean water, the Abbot getting it after all the rest.

Inevitably, I asked about the silence. Was it not a terrible penance, a whole life spent in almost total silence? He smiled again. "Oh, no," he replied. "The young men find it trying, of course; but as one becomes accustomed to it one doesn't mind. Indeed, one comes to like it. It saves so much time."

He paused reflectively, then added, "But I'll tell you what is the real penance, the one that gets more and more irksome as the years go by. It is that you are never alone. We eat together, pray together, work together in the fields, sit together in the study, and, as you have seen, sleep alongside one another in the dormitory. We are *never alone.*"

He let the horror of it sink into my mind. As I pondered it, the quasi-eremitical life of a Carthusian or Camaldolese began to look by comparison almost humane. The Trappist must try to attain spiritual solitude with never a moment physically alone. One need not go so far as to say with Sartre that hell is other people in order to appreciate the ferocity of such a life. No wonder silence seemed to the Prior a trivial restriction.

In the refectory, the tables were set with aluminum plates and implements, a sort of fork-cum-spoon. I noticed that the Abbot's plate was encircled with wildflowers wound together like a daisy chain.

"It happens to be the Abbot's feast day, so we honor him," said the Prior.

Soon it was time for Vespers. Even the abbey church was austere and cold. When I told the Abbot afterwards that I must return to Paris that evening, he expressed astonishment, saying he had expected me to stay at least two weeks. No one before had ever left the same day. I apologized but assured him I must get back that night.

I was escorted to the abbey gate by the guest master. On the way, he told me he had never been to Paris. "I understand it is a very large city," he said in his slow, carefully enunciated French. Then, "Is Scotland a very Catholic country?" Without newspapers or radio, he was more completely cut off from the world than a little child on a prairie farm. He was a priest, so he must have been at least twenty-five, but he talked like a pious boy of ten.

It was almost midnight when my train reached the Gare Mont-parnasse, whence I had set out that morning. The lights of the city blinked and twinkled and trailed. Even in the night air, the familiar Paris smell of cosmetics and cigars, of perfume and garlic, came in occasional whiffs. Could it have been only sixteen hours since I had left Paris? It seemed so many centuries to the Middle Ages and back. And the Abbot's kindly, confident voice was still ringing gently in my ears: "Nous avons la vérité."

Today, life at the Grande Trappe has been considerably modified as a result of changes ordered in the wake of Vatican II. Even Mount Athos is hardly what it was in 1964. Such hallowed places of pilgrimage will remain so long as there is life on our planet. But they will never have quite the flavor I knew. I am glad to have seen them as they were and to have the last echo of the Middle Ages in my ears.

Although both before and after coming to America I met many of the most celebrated Protestant thinkers, I knew few of them well. The first American in this category that I met was Reinhold Niebuhr, with whom I had a few conversations in 1939 in Edinburgh, where also I heard him deliver some of the lectures that were to become famous in their day under the title *The Nature and Destiny of Man*. His genre of politico-religious thought was not much in my line, but his personality was impressive and his presence distinctly powerful.

His utterances from the podium came across in spurts of rapid machine gun fire. Britain was already at war while he was delivering some of these lectures and, on one occasion at least, the crash of bombs was heard. Niebuhr seemed to pay no attention, continuing to extrude his words as if responding to the enemy onslaught. In conversation he was only slightly less aggressive in his style. He gave the impression of feeling himself towering over anyone with whom he spoke. Yet he was friendly in his way.

I met Karl Barth only in a perfunctory way, but later heard him give a lecture in San Francisco. (His son, Markus, a contemporary of mine at divinity school in Edinburgh, accounted his father "not Barthian enough.") Barth, whose personal greatness even a brief encounter immediately disclosed, was emphatically German-Swiss and Pro-testant. Despite the popular image of him, especially in his earlier years, as an aloof Germanic professor full of anti-American prejudices, he was by no means lacking in human sympathy and understanding; nor need one be surprised to learn, as one does from his last autobiographical report in *The Christian Century*, that in his theological study were to be seen hanging pictures of Calvin and

Mozart next to each other and at the same height.

I encountered Paul Tillich only after I came to the United States, where I met him several times, introducing him when he gave a public lecture at Bryn Mawr, and was on a later occasion, entertained by him and Mrs. Tillich in their flat in Chicago. People seemed to understand Tillich in inverse ratio to their own erudition. A freshman at Bryn Mawr asked him an ingenuously simple-sounding question of the sort, "Dr. Tillich, what exactly is God?" To which Tillich replied, in his heavily German way, "Zat iss a goot question," and then poured forth a long exposition that made most of us look more and more puzzled by the minute, while the girl's face grew more and more radiant, as though mysteries that had always perplexed her were unfolding before her eyes with greater and greater clarity.

I wish I had met Rufus Jones, who died just before I came to America to the chair named for him. Quakers have many great virtues, but a sense of humor is not generally accounted one of them. Rufus Jones, however, appears to have been an exception. Many stories are told of him. A favorite is about Dean Inge and him who, being at a conference together, were lodged in the same hotel. Both were noted for their interest in and work on mysticism. Both had difficulty finding their rooms. They kept bumping into one another as they searched all over the hotel. At last, Jones, confronted once again by Inge, this time in the hotel lobby, asked, "Don't you think we had better ask somebody who is *not* a mystic?"

The most Quakerish American Quaker I ever knew well was Henry Joel Cadbury. Born in Philadelphia in 1883, he became one of the foremost biblical scholars in the English-speaking world. When I knew him, he was the Hollis Professor of Divinity at Harvard. He was a Fellow of the American Academy of Arts and Sciences and a member of many other learned bodies. He served faithfully on the American Friends' Service Committee for many years.

Although a most careful and diligent scholar, he had almost no theological sensitivity at all. Asked by a Bryn Mawr undergraduate why Quakers do not have sacraments, he replied simply that sacraments have been the occasion of the major controversies in the Church and that Quakers avoid such controversies by not having sacraments. "You can't fight with anybody over sacraments if you haven't got any," he remarked with cool serenity. Related to the English Cadbury family, he was, as befits a birthright Quaker, a convinced pacifist. If the highest Christian value is the absence of controversy, then perhaps his view on sacraments is unavoidable.

One of the most distinguished biblical scholars in my time at Oxford was Robert Henry Lightfoot, an Etonian who was ordained priest in 1910, was Dean Ireland Professor from 1934 till 1949 and editor of the *Journal of Theological Studies* (in which I wrote an article for him) till his death in 1953. Unlike Austin Farrer, who was openly impatient with much of German biblical scholarship, which he accounted at best ponderous and at worst wrongheaded, Lightfoot was much influenced by the *Formgeschichte* school, whose representatives include Dibelius and Bultmann, causing him to be more than ordinarily skeptical about the historicity of the Gospel narratives. So extreme was his caution that students who came under his influence delighted to parody his utterances. One such parody that I recall ran as follows: "I believe one may go so far as to say, without undue danger of showing a lack of scholarly caution that, so far as the evidence at our disposal permits us to conjecture, the disciple whose name is recorded as Judas was perhaps (indeed one might almost say probably) among the least faithful."

I met Bertrand Russell briefly twice: once in England and once at Haverford College, Pennsylvania. As brilliant in conversation as in his writings and evincing the same puckish and mischievous wit, he always fascinated undergraduates with his iconoclastic thrusts at the sacred cows of Church and State. In 1940, when the College of the City of New York invited Lord Russell to lecture on logic and the philosophy of mathematics and science and Russell accepted, nobody of such eminence had ever been on the faculty of that institution. The invitation had been unanimous on the part of the nineteen members of the governing board that had attended the meeting. When the appointment was made public, William Thomas Manning, Bishop of the Anglican diocese of New York, denounced the board's action on the ground that Russell's writings showed him to be "a recognized propagandist against both religion and morality, and who specifically defends adultery."

The Bishop's attack was the signal for an astonishing campaign of vilification and intimidation. Russell was alluded to in speeches as "The professor of immorality" and the like till almost every civic and religious institution in New York City was reverberating with similar abuse. Borough President Harvey of Queens threatened that if the invitation were not canceled he would move to strike out the next year's appropriation of $7,500,000 for the maintenance of the municipal colleges. At the same meeting, a councilman stated that "if we had an adequate system of immigration, that bum could not land within a thousand miles." Eventually, the board that had invited Russell formally disinvited him.

It happened that Russell, who was, of course, supported by the entire academic and scientific community, had a book coming out, entitled *The Meaning and Nature of Truth*. Since he was far too eminent ever to need to cite anything on the title page other than his name, his readers were astonished to open the book and find an ostentatious array of designations, titles, and awards. The astonishment changed to merriment, of course, when they reached the mischievous satire of the last two lines, in which he set forth his latest honor: "Judicially pronounced unworthy to be Professor of Philosophy at the College of the City of New York (1940)."[4]

Emil Brunner, of the Swiss Reformed Church, was another fashionable Protestant theologian of the period. I was never actually introduced to him, although I did hear one of his lectures at the University of Glasgow in the forties. Like his writings, it was solid and well organized, but even the most charitable would have had to call it unexciting, not to say dull.

Henry Sloane Coffin, who had retired from the presidency of Union Theological Seminary, New York, by the time I came to the United States, was, despite the somewhat robust heaviness of his manner and style, anything other than dull. I had already met him in Glasgow where he was talking to a group of Scottish Presbyterian clergy, one of whom asked a question reflecting a more than ordinary ignorance of American religious life. Coffin had been alluding to the aforementioned bishop, William Thomas Manning, the antagonist in the Bertrand Russell controversy. The questioner in the Glasgow audience wanted to know whether Bishop Manning had jurisdiction over Union Seminary. Coffin had enormous eyebrows and a stentorian voice. The eyebrows shot up as he roared, "God *forbid!*"

My first meeting with Coffin on the other side of the Atlantic was in 1950 at his home in Lakeville, Connecticut, to which he had invited my wife and myself during our stay with Emma Bailey Speer. Coffin had an endless fund of stories, which he told well. He would tell, for instance, of the telephone call he had received while working late one night at the seminary. "Is that Union Ceme-te-ry?" After a long pause, Coffin answered in his most sepulchral tone, "Coffin speaking."

When the afterwards eminent biblical scholar Kirsopp Lake first came to Union, it was the custom to ask the most junior member of the Faculty to say grace. From the head of the table came the booming voice of Coffin, "Doctor Lake, will you say gr-race, please?" And from the other end a shrill, piping English voice, "No, thank you very much, I'd rather not."

Lake, according to Coffin, had no musical sense at all and also accounted an invitation to preach an opportunity to give a technical lecture to a captive audience. Seated in a stall in a great American cathedral in which he was to preach, he heard a chanting noise. Turning to the canon in the next stall he asked, "Sermon hymn?" "Litany, Dr. Lake." Again more noise. "Sermon hymn?" "Anthem, Dr. Lake." Once again, "Sermon hymn?" "No, Ante-Communion," to which Lake responded with a shrill comment that reverberated down the nave, "O my God, this is more than flesh and blood can stand."

Coffin also told of his attending a little fundamentalist bethel in London. Seated in the front row, he heard the Cockney preacher begin, "I am preaching todye on the Hepistle of Syent Paul the Haposthe to the Ebrews. There are some people wot syes the Hepistle of Syent Paul to the Ebrews weren't written by Syent Paul. Well, wot I'd like to know is, if it weren't written by Syent Paul, 'ow did 'e get 'is nyme at the top of it?" So good a raconteur was Coffin that he added a bristle of his own shaggy eyebrows to the punchline. A delightful man of great dignity and old-fashioned wit and wisdom.

In that summer of 1950 when Emma Bailey Speer invited my wife and me with our two small children to her lovely home in Lakeville, Connecticut, she was approaching eighty. Mentally very alert indeed, this remarkable lady was filled with zeal for righteousness and eagerness to continue doing the good deeds she had been doing from the earliest years of her life. Born in 1872, Emma Bailey had gone to Bryn Mawr but had left before graduating, in order to marry Robert Elliott Speer, a Princetonian destined to become very prominent in Presbyterian circles. He was for many years secretary of the Board of Missions of the Presbyterian Church (U.S.A.) and in 1927, Moderator of its General Assembly. Emma, who had become a member of the national board of the Y.W.C.A. in 1906, served as its president from 1915 until 1932, and as its honorary president from 1932 till 1944.

The weeks we spent there in our first summer in the United States were filled with thoughtfulness, quietude, and peace. Like many others coming from Europe to America in the years just after the war, I had vaguely in my mind images of fast-talking salesmen, sassy kids, roaring preachers, and husbands and wives throwing one another out of top-story windows in Manhattan in the course of family tiffs. If any such delusions about American life could have survived my first year at Bryn Mawr, they would have been put to rest by that visit to the household over which Emma Speer so graciously presided. Her leisurely, patrician speech and stately and gentle way of life would have been hard to match at that time anywhere in England. Her ideals were indeed nineteenth-century ones. In spite of changing times, she had been able to retain servants whom she treated with the utmost courtesy and consideration, while insisting that everything be done with the grace and elegance she had known in her youth in Pennsylvania.

Dinner was served every evening with gracious simplicity, yet as correctly as though she were giving a formal dinner party. After dinner, conversation was conducted as if it were an art such as playing the cello or the flute. Then came a somewhat ritualistic game of gin rummy, which she insisted was a most desirable form of relaxation, not least for philistines like myself who in our ignorance account all card games a waste of time. After the cards had been carefully put back in their place, we ensconced ourselves in comfortable armchairs to read, each in his or her turn, from an English or American classic, perhaps Stevenson or Emerson or Dickens, preferably something not too heavy yet thought-provoking and in some way fortifying to the soul. Finally came the most completely indispensable rite of all, family prayers.

There was a strong Quaker element in her outlook and I understand she did have Quaker ancestry. She certainly had in an eminent degree the Quaker concern for justice along with the ideal of a life of cultured simplicity. Her outward allegiance, however, was unreservedly to the Presbyterian Church and on Sundays she faithfully attended its services.

In the afternoons, the chauffeur would drive us all at a gentle speed around the neighboring countryside, stopping perhaps for a few minutes to make a purchase at an old-fashioned store and exchange civilities with its owner. The children were encouraged to play independently with a handsome supply of equipment provided for that purpose (she had had children and grandchildren of her own, including a daughter who was for many years Headmistress of Shipley, one of the foremost girls' schools in the United States), but they always joined us at meals. Conversation at table was skillfully geared in part to their interests, yet directed in such a way as to encourage them to enjoy their elders' concerns.

On the grounds of the house was a separate building that she affectionately called Iona, where was housed her husband's large and important library, now the Robert E. Speer Wing of the library of Princeton Theological Seminary, as she had for long arranged that it would become. From the old world ambience in which she lived, the tempo of modern life was startlingly alien.

Some men eschew controversy as meretricious and vulgar, while others, no less gifted and sincere, welcome it as a good soldier welcomes the fray and scars of battle. Jim Pike, an American Anglican Bishop, was certainly of the latter class—fortunately for him, since he never needed to court it. He had only to land in a foreign country as an unheralded nobody and within a week he would be on the front page, with tongues wagging everywhere. His flair for controversy made him capable of quite naturally raising in sermons questions that are habitually raised by trained theologians but cause consternation in the temples of non-think. These propensities eventually, not to say inevitably, led to his near expulsion by the House of Bishops, who for prudential reasons restrained their ire to the extent of letting him retain a voice in their assemblies while depriving him of his seat. In response to this action, he publicly quipped, "You'll wish you had given me a seat and no voice!"

I knew Jim in my Bryn Mawr days, when he was Dean of the Cathedral of St. John the Divine in New York. He ran a program on television (then in its infancy as a public communication medium) in which he, his wife Esther, and their small children would sit around the fireside and engage in intelligent talk about religion. The talk might seem a trifle contrived when an almost baby voice would suddenly pipe up, "But Daddy, aren't you forgetting about the Hypostatic Union?" To the many viewers accustomed to religious pap who had not unnaturally hitherto supposed that the use of the human brain in religion is strictly forbidden, these telecasts must have been infinitely beneficial. He came annually to speak at Bryn Mawr, whose students (admitted on a ratio of about one in fifteen ambitious applicants to work under a faculty that included some of the internationally foremost authorities in their fields) enjoyed his straightforward and lucid style and intelligent presentations. I often dropped in on him in New York to enjoy his friendly and challenging converse over a glass of sherry.

We went to the west coast about the same time and were close in age. He went to San Francisco as Bishop of the Diocese there; I went to Los Angeles as Dean of the Graduate School of Religion at USC. I often flew to San Francisco for meetings such as those of the Pacific Coast Theological Society, which were held, in those days, in the Chapter House Library of Grace Cathedral, so I sometimes dropped into his office there. He would whisk me inside to a scene in which, typically, he would be dictating to a secretary one minute and into a machine the next, while chainsmoking with one hand and munching a chocolate bar in the other; moving now and then to the telephone and intermittently engaging me in intellectually provocative converse.

After his son's tragic suicide in England, I noticed the cathedral precincts crowded with row upon row of little-boy acolytes in their soutanes of various colors according to the parishes whence they had come. Jim, whom I discovered alone in his office, insisted that I come in so long as I did not mind his undressing as we talked, whereupon he divested himself of all but the undershorts and ended up in a cope and mitre, talking incessantly all the while. I remarked that I could not stay for the service since I had a plane to catch, and he grinned, "Oh, pity you can't stay for the Holy Show!"

Distraught as he was at this time by his son's death, he was as intellectually alive as always and, if possible, even more openminded than ever, eagerly exploring parapsychology and other areas the Church likes to account more suspect than mental sloth. The fact that we did not by any means always share the same opinions made no more difference to our friendship than if one of us had preferred muffins for breakfast and the other toast. As a member of the House of Bishops, he must have seemed to many onlookers as unlikely as a Wimbledon champion at a suburban ping-pong party.

For many years, I have enjoyed the privilege of knowing many Jewish friends of high intellectual calibre and warm disposition. Many of them, happily, are still alive. Among those now deceased, three very different men spring to mind.

One is Nelson Glueck, a man of prodigious energy and immense accomplishment in several ways even apart from his own field of archaeology. When I met him, he was president of the four-campus institution known all over the world as the center of rabbinical studies in the tradition of the Reformed branch of Judaism: Hebrew Union. I was fortunate enough to be with him on a dig in Israel in 1964 where I saw him in many ways at his best, for he loved nothing better than pursuing his work in the Negev that had brought him much fame in scholarly circles. He had discovered King Solomon's copper mines in the Wadi Arabah and had directed the excavations of Ezion-geber (Solomon's seaport on the Red Sea) and elsewhere. He had also served the United States in the Middle East in wartime with the Office of Strategic Services.

He was not a ritually observant Jew, nor was he by any reckoning an original theologian or the architect of new ideas for Judaism. He was at his best as a scientist and as a practical administrator, although he tended to be bored with details. Widely accounted something of a *prima donna*, he could be imperious, but much was forgiven him for he was indubitably a truly great man.

I met Martin Buber in Jerusalem a few months before he died. He was then in his mid-eighties. He was, by that time, by no means as easy to talk to as one might expect of the author of *Ich und Du*, a study of personal relationship.[5] Perhaps like many elderly people, he had developed a suspicion of his fellow men. At any rate, he seemed to treat even the most straightforward and innocent questions with such suspicion that one began to feel that if one had inquired about the weather he would have suspected an ulterior motive. It was just as this atmosphere of suspicion had reached its zenith and most of us, Jews and Gentiles, were searching in our minds for something particularly innocuous to say that a Southern Baptist at the back of the room asked very earnestly in a luscious, South Carolina drawl, "Tell me, Doctor Buber, what do you think of Jesus Chrehst?"

The horror swept through the old philosopher's living room like a sudden discharge of electricity. There was a long pause during which one could all but hear the unspoken prayers of Jews and Christians fervently uniting on lines such as "Adonai, don't let him hear it" and perhaps even "Lord, may the earth open and swallow us all up." At length, the aged voice replied, "That is a very *general* question. I can answer only *specific* questions."

That was that. Later, however, after we had all recovered our composure, I did manage to extract from him the information that the basic concept of his *Ich und Du* had come to him in the trenches in World War I, when he had been fighting on the German side. Rather short in stature with soulful eyes, he was an impressive personality even in the bedroom slippers in which his feet were shod.

David Ben Gurion, the third in my Jewish triad, was one of the most impressive human beings I have ever met. A former head of state, he talked with disarming simplicity and lovable openness. Although he was nearly eighty when I met him in Israel, his blue eyes shone with an unusual clarity and his shock of white hair seemed to stand up in sheer surprise above his warm, florid face at the wonder of the world about him. He looked at you as if he truly loved you for being human. To desert dwellers, water has naturally a very special importance and he talked a little about it. "The Bible," he said, "promises a land flowing with milk and honey. It says nothing about water." The ardor of his Zionist views made him controversial, but Jews all over the world should be proud to have had Judaism represented by such a splendid human being.

Among distinguished French philosophers of a bygone generation, I met Etienne Gilson, Jacques Maritain, and Gabriel Marcel, each only once. Both Maritain and Marcel, although charming in their way, gave the impression of being a trifle vain, *légèrement vaniteux*. Not so Gilson, whose knowledge of medieval thought was staggering but who could also talk with wit and verve on many subjects. He had enormous energy, enjoyed fine wines, and lived in good health and spirits to the age of ninety-four.

It is always interesting to have known or even met people who at the time were not particularly well known and who later became famous. Soon after my arrival in the United States in 1949, I was dining in a private home in Boston at which the only other dinner guest was Paul Dudley White, who later became much celebrated as President Eisenhower's personal physician and heart specialist. A spare man who obviously practiced what he preached about exercise and diet, he was a very interesting and informative conversationalist. He was making a study, at that time, of the correlation between the incidence of heart disease in various Italian cities and the various ways in which they cooked spaghetti, for since each region has its own culinary traditions, he believed he could establish reliable scientific findings on the relation between diet and heart trouble. I never met him again.

Nor did I ever again meet Martin Luther King, Jr., after a brief encounter with him in Los Angeles in the late fifties. King was already a very notable black Baptist minister at that time, but he had not then attained anything like the fame he was to acquire some years later, let alone the unique place he won posthumously in the hearts of millions. There was something so casual about him that made him seem less the politico-religious leader he was then soon to become than the almost anonymous embodiment of the people he was so effectively to represent before his tragic assassination.

In 1951, somewhat exhausted after the *soutenance* for my doctorate at the Sorbonne, I remained in Europe for some weeks to unwind by visiting friends in France, Italy, and Belgium. It was during the unlikely circumstance of staying at the house of a Waldensian lady in Rome, with whom I had lodged as a student in the thirties, that I had the honor of an *udienza speciale*[6] with Pius XII at the papal summer palace at Castelgandolfo, on August 21. I happened to be talking to a friend at the American Embassy in Rome (I was still a British subject, not then an American citizen, though I had been already living for two years in the United States) who seemed impressed by my knowledge of Vatican affairs.

Suddenly, he asked, "Would you like to meet the Pope?" I said yes, but it would be impossible, since I was to be in Rome for only another few days. He made a couple of telephone calls and returned to say that, if I would go immediately to a certain convent and identify myself, the sisters would have an invitation for me to be received in special audience the following morning at nine o'clock. There would be about a dozen at the audience, but I should have an opportunity for some conversation with His Holiness. Also, it would mean rather an early start, for the summer palace is about twenty miles out of Rome.

Castelgandolfo, the seat of the Savelli in the Middle Ages, has belonged to the popes since 1596. The summer palace was erected by Urban VIII from designs by Carlo Moderna and stands on a splendid site high above the Lake of Albano which, nearly a thousand feet above sea level and nearly five hundred feet deep, is formed by the crater of an extinct volcano. The lake is about six miles in circumference and, fed by copious subterranean springs, is drained by a very ancient *emissarium*, an outlet that issues below Castelgandolfo. The summer palace provides welcome relief from the oppressive, humid heat of Rome, which at that season is usually all but unbearable.

In 1870, when the First Vatican Council was being protracted by the learned and lengthy disquisitions of those prelates who opposed the concept of papal infallibility, the summer heat of Rome caused some of them to take ill and then to request postponement till they could return. Cardinal Antonelli pointed out, however, that these prelates, many of them from northern countries and unaccustomed to such heat, need not have taken ill had they not protracted the debate by arguing against papal infallibility, contrary to the express wishes of the Holy Father, Pius IX. The Pope, according to one story, is said to have exclaimed, when he had heard the objection that these northern prelates would be dying off like flies in the heat: *Che crepino pure!* "Just let them die!" Be that as it may, by the time of my encounter with the papacy eighty-one years later, a very different pontiff was reigning.

The audience chamber was hushed as we awaited in silence the Pope's arrival. We were all clad in more or less sombre clothes, the ladies wearing long black dresses, most with the lace mantilla preferred for such occasions. Apart from myself, the dozen or so in the audience chamber were divided into small family or other groups, with two to four persons in each. Despite the early hour and the elevated situation of Castelgandolfo, the morning air was already warm though not oppressive like Rome. All faces looked expectantly toward the end of the room where the pontiff was to appear. On some was a slight smile of contentment that Providence had brought them hither.

Suddenly, the lone white figure of Pius XII appeared and strode out counterclockwise round the chamber. Eugenio Pacelli, who had been elected on March 2, 1939, contrary to a tradition against electing the papal secretary of state (his position at that time), was immensely impressive. Aristocratic both by lineage and in demeanor, he seemed to exude an air of calm, princely holiness and intense dedication to his papal office.

I was standing at about the middle of the group. As he approached me, I became more aware of the darkness and leanness of his face. He talked in good English. Although much papal English is traditionally limited to benisons and the like, rather than for more intricate human communication, his was that of an accomplished linguist and of a diplomat of the old school.

He spoke with great seriousness. When I mentioned that I was not a Roman Catholic, he was quick to say, "Nevertheless, I welcome you—and bless you." I told him I had recently gone to a professorial chair in America. "A beautiful profession," he observed. His manner was friendly, in a cool, dignified way, and above all priestly. We spoke briefly of the state of the world and he made studiously noncommittal comments. Despite his priestliness, there was almost no vestige of pastoral concern for any of us till he returned to his original place on a dais at the end of the chamber. Then he seemed to turn into a simple parish priest as he invited those of us who had rosaries and other religious objects (*oggetti religiosi*) that they wished to have blessed to hold them up, whereupon he uttered blessings and prayers with an air of fatherly affection but most of all conveying a sense of his own awareness of his position as the center and focus of the whole Church.

He had a personal aura that was very distinctive. In the course of his career in ecclesiastical diplomacy, before his election as pope, he had scored many successes. His concordat in 1933 with National Socialist Germany, controversial from the beginning, had become much more so during his pontificate in wartime. Whatever be the truth about the labyrinthine relationships into which his diplomatic maneuvers took him, and as much as his style of pontificate differed from that of his successor, John XXIII, his personal dedication to his office was very striking and his personality unique.

I have never met any other popes. In 1964, however, when I was staying for a few days with the Abbot General of the Premonstratensians (Monseigneur Norbert Calmels) at their house in the Viale Giotto, he expressed his regret that he could not arrange, as he would have wished, for me to have an audience with Paul VI at such short notice but, if I cared to accompany him the following morning, June 28, to be at St. Peter's at seven o'clock, where the Pope was to consecrate four bishops, he would see that I had a good seat. So the following morning, I found myself in a car approaching the Basilica. In the company of the Abbot General, I found all doors seemed to open by magic at the wave of his hand and soon I was ensconced in a seat within talking distance of the procession. When the short, portly figure of Monseigneur Calmels hove into sight he glanced over and threw me a gesture of satisfaction at the place I had been assigned.

At length, Paul VI appeared, amid exuberant cries of *Viva il Papa*. An earnest man though no doubt he was, he did not have anything like the distinctiveness of Pius XII, whose passing had marked the end of a papal era. Charisma is, after all, a very personal gift.

In recording these miscellaneous encounters with interesting people in this chapter I have probably forgotten some, perhaps many, who should have been mentioned. One, however, I dare not omit, even though it was especially casual and brief. In 1950, soon after my wife and I had came with our two small children to the United States, Andrew Mutch, a dear eighty-year old Scot who had come to America in 1911 as Minister of the Bryn Mawr Presbyterian Church and was now retired, proposed to drive us all to Princeton for a day's visit to that lovely campus. He still spoke with a thick Perthshire speech that caused Philadelphia businessmen to ask him goodnaturedly why he had never lost it in all these years. With a twinkle in his loving and laughing eyes, he would say, "Mebbe I couldna affor-r-rd to lose it." He was what the Scots in earlier times called "pawky," an untranslatable Scots word, with connotations that include shrewdness, caution, artfulness, and a very dry but kindly and special sense of humor. He was also singularly tolerant and compassionate, with a great generosity of spirit. Before we set out he said he would like to offer a "wee prayer-r" for his careful driving and our safe return.

As we passed through one of the buildings at Princeton, I noticed two men sitting in a dark alcove. "Oh, let's just stop for a wee minute," whispered Andrew. "I see somebody I would like ye to meet." We followed him into the dimness where suddenly I perceived that, without a shadow of a doubt, I was facing Albert Einstein, seated and wearing the celebrated navy blue sweater.

"I would like ye to meet my friends," said Mutch in his best homespun. Einstein beamed pleasantly. Courtesies were exchanged and we resumed our walk through the campus.

Einstein, for all his intellectual genius, was as disarmingly warmhearted as Andrew Mutch himself. A little girl who lived in Princeton came back from school very late one afternoon. Her mother naturally demanded an explanation. At last the child confessed that she had been having a lot of trouble with her arithmetic and, since she had heard that Mr. Einstein was very good at it, she called on him and asked if he would help her with her homework. The mother, in consternation, then called Einstein with profuse apologies for her daughter's intrusion.

"No," Einstein had replied. "I am grateful to your little daughter. She showed me something in the mathematical theory of numbers that I had not thought of before." Out of such humility of heart springs the openmindedness of authentic genius.

Andrew Mutch, who lived to the age of ninety-three, was still annually reading the Christmas lesson at the Bryn Mawr College Chapel as he had done for many decades. The last time I heard him, he stumbled slightly over the second last verse.

"Oh dear-r," he sighed afterwards from an armchair in our home where my wife was plying him with refreshments. "I am r-really ashamed of myself this night. I made a terrible mess of it. They'll never-r ask me back."

Andrew Mutch, even at the age of ninety, still did not know how much he was beloved. When you think of it, neither did any of the characters celebrated in this book know it of themselves. That is a large part of the secret of their lovability. For once you know how good you are, your knowledge spoils your goodness. It is when you do not know it that you become as lovable as a little child and so capture everybody's heart.

Acknowledgments

I wish to thank the following persons and institutions for their courtesies and help:

The British Academy, which lent me the photograph of Austin Farrer, and Studio Edmark, London, for their kind permission to use it; Dr. E.W. Christie, St. Andrews, Scotland, for a photograph and handwriting of Miss Christie, and Maurice Fleming, Iain Flett, and the *Dundee Courier* for enabling me to find him; Father Francis Edwards, S.J., Archivist for the English Province of his Society, who provided the photograph of Father D'Arcy and put at my disposal certain material normally accessible only to members of that Society; Professor Emerita Dorothy Emmet, University of Manchester, for leading me to her colleague Dr. D.P. Henry, who generously presented me with the rare photograph of A.D. Ritchie (rare because Ritchie's characteristic modesty had resulted in his apparently never having had a professional one taken throughout his life, so that neither Manchester nor Edinburgh University had been able to supply one); the Master of Balliol (Christopher Hill) for comment on Arthur Marder's year in the Eastman Chair at Oxford; Mrs. Jan Marder for the photograph and handwriting of her late husband; Mrs. Margaret Ramsey for her late husband's photograph; Mrs. Katharine Ritchie for information on her late husband's early life; the Scottish National Portrait Gallery for the photograph of John Gray, which is reproduced by their kind permission, and Paul Winckler by whose kind permission the handwritten letter of John Gray is reproduced; and the Very Reverend Ronald Selby Wright for the photograph of Charles Warr greeting the Queen, both attired in the robes of the Order of the Thistle, and the *Glasgow Herald* for their kind permission to use it.

My gratitude goes also to others who have either helped me in researching data or responded to my sometimes importunate inquiries. These include Miss Jessie Baxter; Canon Ronald Head, Oxford; Dr. S.V. Lenkey, Stanford University; Mrs. Bridget Molloy, Librarian of the School of Philosophy, University of Southern California, and her colleagues Miss Marion Schulman and Dr. Ross Scimeca; the Reverend Professor Emeritus Eric Mascall, Canon of Truro; Mrs. Jean A. Munro; Mrs. Joan Scott; and Father Brocard Sewell, Order of the Carmelites.

To Allan W. Campbell, Edinburgh, for his reading of much of the manuscript and for his scholarly criticisms along the way, as well as for suggesting the book in the first place and for innumerable kindnesses to me in recent years, I owe a debt of gratitude that not even my dedication of the book to him can redress. He, like some other living friends of mine, is ineligible for inclusion among the subjects of my book only because I insist on previous death as a requirement for even such private canonization as I presume to undertake. I cannot but rejoice, therefore, that such friends are so disqualified.

Geddes MacGregor

Chapter Notes

NOTES TO CHAPTER ONE

1. Post-Vatican II modifications have diminished the beauty of the interior but much remains.
2. The opening words of Vespers: "O God, come to my aid."
3. Peter Anson, *A Roving Recluse*, (Cook, Ireland: Mercier Press, 1946) 142.
4. Bruce Marshall, the Scottish novelist born a decade later, once told me that his conversion was set in similar circumstances, giving him the sense of God's having chosen ugly, ungainly, and unlikely men to be the channels of his saving grace—vessels of clay showing that the power is God's, not theirs.
5. Father Brocard Sewell informs me that this was discovered by Professor James G. Nelson.
6. Brocard Sewell, *Footnote to the Nineties*, (London: Cecil and Amelia Woolf, 1968) 10. For a variety of pieces on Gray, see the John Gray Commemorative number of *The Aylesford Review*, edited by the English Carmelites at Aylesford Priory, near Maidenstone, Kent, IV:2 (Spring 1961).
7. H.P. Clive, *Pierre Louÿs* (Oxford: Clarendon Press, 1978) 81f. There is a study of the relation between Louÿs and another of his friends by Robert Fleury, *Pierre Louÿs et Gilbert de Voisins: une curieuse amitié* (Paris: Editions Tête de Feuilles, 1973). On the friendship between Louÿs and Gray, see also Roger Lhombreaud, "Une amitié anglaise de Pierre Louÿs," in *Revue de Littérature Comparée*, XXVII (1953) 343-357, and Peter Vernon, "John Gray's Letters to Pierre Louÿs," in *Revue de Littérature Comparée*, LIII (1979) 88-107.
8. *Blackfriars*, 10 (1929) 779-785. Raffalovich used the pseudonym of Alexander Michaelson.
9. *The Tablet*, 223 (October 25, 1969) 1042f.
10. Verlaine (1844-1896) was the son of one of Napoleon's soldiers. With his friend Jean Arthur Rimbaud, he roamed France and England. For shooting his friend (fortunately with bad aim) he was imprisoned for two years.
11. "Smudge of the Cross": a reminder that we are dust and unto dust we shall return.
12. This church, a strange, octagonal building dating from 1865, had in earlier years served as a Victorian place of popular entertainment. In 1940, it was seriously damaged in an air raid but after the war was restored by artists from all over France, including Jean Cocteau who, in 1960, contributed a mural depicting the Crucifixion with strongly occult overtones.

NOTES TO CHAPTER THREE

1. Sixteen was at that time not at all an unusual age for university admission.
2. "Ah, Reverend Father, you have returned from the African Missions?"
3. "You know, these churchmen go to colleges and their heads expand."

NOTES TO CHAPTER FOUR

1. Later published as *Aesthetic Experience in Religion* (London: Macmillan & Co., Ltd., 1947).
2. In American terms, it was science at the level of a high school sophomore.

NOTES TO CHAPTER FIVE

1. Philosophical studies at the Scottish universities were divided into two categories, corresponding roughly to Aristotle's ancient distinction between *theoria* and *praxis*.
2. *Essays in Philosophy and Other Pieces* (London: Longmans Green, 1948).
3. *Ibid.*, 30.
4. *George Berkeley: A Reappraisal* (Manchester: Manchester University Press, 1967).

Ritchie died on March 12, 1967. It was edited with a preface by George Davie and with the help of Professor Dorothy Emmet and Katharine Ritchie.

NOTES TO CHAPTER SIX

1. Some of the biographical background here comes from David L. Edwards, *Ian Ramsey, Bishop of Durham* (London:Oxford University Press, 1973). Dedicated to Ian's widow, it contains, as an appendix, the text of a memorial address delivered in St. Margaret's, Westminster, by Michael Ramsey, Archbishop of Canterbury, on November 17, 1972. For the benefit of readers unfamiliar with the English scene, let it be noted that there was no family relationship between the two Ramseys, who came out of quite different backgrounds.
2. Included in his writings were the trilogy, *Religious Language* (1957), *Models and Mystery* (1964), and *Christian Discourse* (1965). Only the first was out when he taught the summer course at my university in California. I remember how annoyed he was, when I paid my first visit to his home in Oxford, that he did not have a copy of *Christian Discourse* to give me. My copy contains a 3½ x 4½ inch memo in his tiny handwriting, dated July 26, 1965, the first paragraph of which reads:

   My dear Geddes,
   After telephone calls and various notes I've managed to bully OUP into sending me a copy of *Christian Discourse* which I'm sending on to you so that you'll have it before you leave [England].

   How typical both of his thoughtfulness and of his punctiliousness in detail! He always followed up even the slightest hint of a promise.
3. In Warren E. Steinkraus, ed., *New Studies in Berkeley's Philosophy* (New York: Holt, Rinehart and Winston, 1966). The article is a revision of a contribution he made at the International Congress of Philosophy in 1953 and a sermon preached that year at the Berkeleian Commemoration at Trinity College, Dublin.
4. John Milton, *Lycidas*.
5. Alexander Pope, *Epilogue to the Satires*, Dialogue II.
6. That is, the old *Bradshaw's Railway Companion*.
7. On our first visit, in 1969, my wife and I slept in a bed in which Queen Victoria had slept before her accession to the British throne. It had been rebuilt, however, after its collapse under the weight of an archbishop of Canterbury who had subsequently occupied it.

NOTES TO CHAPTER SEVEN

1. Many Scots still maintain that instinctive dread of English and American speech. It is said that when George, the fourth earl of Aberdeen, returned from schooldays at Harrow and the "grand tour" of Europe (having attained his majority in 1805), an old huntsman remarked that the new laird would have been a fine man "gin they hadna ta'en him to England and spoiled his education." So one can understand Jim's solicitude for Alice, even in the first moments of their conversation.
2. Example of Glasgow "Cockney": a little boy and his parents are in a rowboat on the River Clyde. While his father is at the oars, the boy says, "Poopahpoo. If ye dinna wanna poopah, let mahpoopah." Translation: "Row, father, row. If you don't want to row, father, let mother row, father."

NOTES TO CHAPTER EIGHT

1. The system was later modified to include a third doctorate, standing between the "big" and the "little" ones. Much more recently, further changes have been made.
2. "I am not a philosopher." He was an *angliciste*—an English literature scholar.
3. "Oh, you are joking!"

NOTE TO CHAPTER NINE

1. Translation:

   What's the use of hoary curls
      Of the bays undying,
   If you cannot kiss the girls
      And drink while time is flying?

NOTE TO CHAPTER ELEVEN

1. The "and dot" bit was even then old-fashioned, representing the sign "&" which in old charts was often found at the end of the alphabet, followed by a period. The tradition has its roots in the hornbook that children carried with them to school—a practice that flourished from the end of the fifteenth century into the eighteenth. I own a form of one in brass, inscribed with the name of St. Paul's School, London, and dated 1729.

NOTES TO CHAPTER TWELVE

1. G. K. Chesterton, *Poems* (London:Burns and Oates, Ltd., 1917) 87-89.
2. G. M. Trevelyan, *History of England* (London: Longmans Green, 1926) 231f.
3. Chesterton, 120-4.
4. Bertrand Russell, *An Inquiry Into the Meaning and Nature of Truth*, (London: George Allen and Unwin, Ltd., 1940).
5. There is an English translation by Walter Kaufmann: Martin Buber, *I and Thou* (New York: Scribners, 1970).
6. In a public audience, the Pope receives a usually vast throng of people; in a private audience, one person alone. In a special audience (*udienza speciale*) he sees a small group.

Arthur Marder

" I suspect that good teaching really consists in spreading a kind of contagion. A good teacher is by way of being an intellectual Typhoid Mary ".

Geddes MacGregor

Bibliographies

BOOKS BY JOHN GRAY

Editor's note: This and the bibliographies appended to the other chapters contain some of the respective authors' more important works. They do not purport to be complete.

Silverpoints, 1893. Poems in a limited edition of 250 numbered copies.
The Blue Calendar, 1895, 1896, 1897, 1898. Sonnets praising saints, carols and other poems; printed privately and issued to friends at Christmas.
Spiritual Poems, 1896. Eleven original poems and twenty-nine translations.
Fourteen Scenes in the Life of the Virgin Mary, 1903. Privately printed; reprinted as *Ad Matrem*.
Ad Matrem, 1904. Issued in several editions.
Verses for Tableaux Vivants, 1905. Sixteen poems; like most of Gray's early works, very rare; Blackwell's Catalogue A25 lists a copy at 300 pounds.
Vivis: poems, 1923. Fifty copies, St. Dominic's Press, Ditchling.
On Hymn Writing, 1925.
St. Peter's, Edinburgh, 1925. A description of the church and its furnishings, including a note on its having been proposed on February 16, 1905, in a vineyard at Marino, Italy, then designed by Sir Robert Lorimer, and the first stone blessed on April 17, 1906.
St. Peter's Hymns, 1925.
Sound, 1926. A poem.
The Long Road, 1926. Poems, including the title poem: The Flying Fish.
Poems, 1931.
Park: A Fantastic Story, 1932. Two hundred fifty copies; printed by René Hague and Eric Gill; devotional work, published posthumously.
A Phial, 1954. A poem that had appeared in *The Venture*, 1903; now reprinted posthumously in an edition of 25 copies.
The Person in Question, 1958. A short story, the manuscript of which was found among Gray's papers and published posthumously in Buenos Aires.

Note: Gray, a prolific writer, contributed extensively to journals and other works. For a bibliography, see G.A. Cevasco, "John Gray (1866-1934): A primary bibliography and an annotated bibliography of writings about him," in *English Literature in Transition, 1880-1920*, 19 (1976), and Ian Fletcher, "Amendments and Additions to a bibliography of John Gray," in *English Literature in Transition, 1880-1920*, 22 (1979). Gray also translated many poems from the French and, perhaps less predictably, some of the writings of Nietzsche.

The literature on Gray and his circle is vast and growing. It includes the following valuable studies:

Anson, Peter F., *A Roving Recluse*. Cork, Ireland: Mercier Press, 1946. Pages 157-161 contain impressions of Gray).
The Aylesford Review, IV:2 (Spring 1961). A special John Gray commemorative number.
Campbell, A.W. (editor), *A Friendship of the Nineties: Letters Between John Gray and Pierre Louÿs*. Edinburgh, Scotland: The Tragara Press, 1984.
Cevasco, G.A., *John Gray*. Boston: Twayne (English Author Series), 1983. This recent work is particularly useful on the literary career of John Gray. It also contains a selected bibliography.

Croft-Cooke, Rupert, *Feasting With Panthers*. London: W.H. Allen, 1967. Chapter 9 consists of an essay entitled "Wilde, Gray and Raffalovich."

Hart-Davis, Rupert, *The Letters of Oscar Wilde*. London, 1962. Contains some references to John Gray by Wilde, and other relevant allusions.

Sewell, Brocard, O. Carm., *Footnote to the Nineties: a Memoir of John Gray and André Raffalovich*. London: Cecil and Amelia Woolf, 1968. Illustrated; contains much interesting material on Gray.

———, *In the Dorian Mode*. Padstow, Cornwall: Tabb House, 1983. This, at the time of writing, is the best book on Gray. See review by Geddes MacGregor in *BookWorld*, XXV:3, 1 (1984), pp. 18 f.

———, ed., "Some Memories of John Gray, by Dominic Hart." *Innes Review* (1975).

———, ed., *Two Friends: John Gray and André Raffalovich*. Aylesford, Kent: Saint Albert's Press, 1963. Contains various essays, a bibliography, and three letters from Raffalovich.

Professor Ruth Z. Temple cites a letter by John Gray (January 20, 1908) in which he corrects the date of his birth as registered by his parents, saying it was in fact March 9, 1866 (R.Z.Temple, "The Other Choice" in *Bulletin of Research in the Humanities*, vol. 84 number 1 (Spring, 1981), p. 19).

BOOKS BY CHARLES WARR

The Unseen Host, 1916. Impressions of World War I; went into ten editions.

Echoes of Flanders, 1916. Another book of war stories based on his personal experiences.

Alfred Warr of Rosneath, 1917. A memoir of his father.

Principal Caird, 1926. A biography of John Caird, a noted philosopher and theologian of his day and Principal of the University of Glasgow.

The Call of the Island, 1929. A novel about the West Highlands of Scotland.

Scottish Sermons and Addresses, 1930.

The Presbyterian Tradition, 1933. A defense of Presbyterian polity and practice.

The Glimmering Landscape, 1960. Autobiographical memoir containing much interesting information about royalty and notable contemporaries.

Editor's note: There is a portrait of Charles Warr by A. E. Borthwick in St. Giles' Cathedral, and a bust by Diana Murray in the Canongate Kirk, Edinburgh.

BOOKS BY DUNCAN MACGREGOR

The Scald, 1874. A poem with which he had entertained his fellow undergraduates at Aberdeen and that ran into two editions.

Clouds and Sunlight, 1884. A book of poems.

Early Scottish Worship, 1896. Lee Lecture, Edinburgh.

Saint Columba, 1897. A portrait of the man who, in the sixth century, founded a monastic establishment at Iona, it contains also translations of some of Columba's hymns and other writings.

BOOKS BY AUSTIN FARRER

Finite and Infinite, 1943. His most difficult work, but also one that reveals the unique philosophical acumen and theological sensitivity of his mind.
The Glass of Vision, 1948. Bampton Lectures.
A Rebirth of Images, 1949.
A Study in St. Mark, 1951.
The Crown of the Year, 1952.
Lord, I Believe, 1955.
The Freedom of the Will, 1958. Gifford Lectures.
Said or Sung, 1960.
Love Almighty and Ills Unlimited, 1961. On the problem of evil.
Commentary on the Revelation of St. John, 1964.
Saving Belief, 1964.
A Science of God?, 1966.
Faith and Speculation, 1967.
A Celebration of Faith, 1970. This and the following works were all posthumously published.
Reflective Faith, 1972.
The End of Man, 1973.
The Brink of Mystery, 1976.
Interpretation and Belief, 1976.

Works on Austin Farrer include:

Curtis, Philip, *A Hawk Among Sparrows: a Biography of Austin Farrer.* London: S.P.C.K., 1985.
Hefling, Charles C., Jr., *Jacob's Ladder: Theology and Spirituality in the Thought of Austin Farrer.* 1979.
See also the article on Farrer by I.M. Crombie in the *Dictionary of National Biography.*

BOOKS BY A. D. RITCHIE

Scientific Method, 1923.
Comparative Physiology of Muscular Tissue, 1928.
Natural History of Mind, 1936.
Civilization, Science and Religion, 1945.
Science and Politics, 1947.
Essays in Philosophy, 1948. Contains his paper, previously published in 1937, "Errors of Logical Positivism," a classic critique of the first edition of A. J. Ayer's *Language, Truth and Logic.*
Studies in the History and Methods of the Sciences, 1958.
George Berkeley: A Reappraisal, 1967. Edited by G. E. Davie, into whose hands Ritchie, when his health was failing, had put the manuscript, calling it his "posthumous book."

BOOKS BY IAN RAMSEY

Miracles: an Exercise in Logical Mapwork, 1952.
Religious Language, 1957.
Freedom and Immortality, 1960.
On Being Sure in Religion, 1963.
Models and Mystery, 1964. Whidden Lectures, McMaster University.
Science and Religion: Conflict and Synthesis, 1964.
Christian Discourse, 1965. Riddell Memorial Lectures, University of Newcastle-on-Tyne.

Books edited by Ian Ramsey

Reasonableness of Christianity [John Locke], 1958.
Prospect for Metaphysics, 1961.
Words about God: the Philosophy of Religion, 1971.

Works on Ian Ramsey include:

Edwards, David L., *Ian Ramsey, Bishop of Durham: A Memoir*. London: Oxford University Press, 1973.

BOOKS BY JAMES T. CLELAND

The True and Lively Word, 1954.
Wherefore Art Thou Come?, 1961.
Preaching to Be Understood, 1965.
He Died as He Lived, 1966.

BOOKS BY RENE LE SENNE

Introduction à la philosophie, 1921. Published in a revised form in several later editions.
Le devoir, 1930.
Le mensonge et le caractère, 1930.
Obstacle et valeur, 1934.
Traité de morale générale, 1942.
Traite de caractérologie, 1945.
La destinée personelle, 1951.
La découverte de Dieu, 1955. Published posthumously.

Works on Le Senne include:

Guzzo, A., G. Clava, C. Rosso, and M. Ghio, *René Le Senne*, 1951.
Paumen, Jean, *Le spiritualisme de René Le Senne [Humanisme et philosophie]*, 1949.
Pirlot, J. *Destinée et valeur. La philosophie de René Le Senne*, 1954.
Sentineo, E., *René Le Senne*, 1953.

A special volume of *Les Etudes philosophiques* (nouvelle série, no. 3) 1955:361-566; Presses Universitaires de France, is devoted to Le Senne, with contributions by M. Barzin, F. Battaglia, A. Devaux, Vl. Jankelevitch, P. Levert, G. MacGregor, G. Marcel, J. Marias, Ch. Perelman, L. de Raeymaeker, A. Reymond, F. J. von Rintelem, M. F. Sciacca, and H. W. Schneider, and studies by G. Berger, F. Brunner, A. Forest, A. Guzzo, R. Maistriaux, P. Mesnard, E. Morot-Sir, and J. Nabert.

BOOKS BY MARTIN D'ARCY

The Mass and the Redemption, 1926.
Catholicism, 1927.
Christ as Priest and Redeemer, 1928.
The Spirit of Charity, 1929.
Thomas Aquinas, 1930.

The Nature of Belief, 1931, 1958.
Mirage and Truth, 1935.
Christian Morals, 1937.
Death and Life, 1942.
Belief and Reason, 1944.
The Mind and Heart of Love, 1945.
Communism and Christianity, 1956.
The Meeting of Love and Knowledge, 1957.
The Sense of History, 1959.
No Absent God, 1962.
Facing God, 1966.
Facing the Truth, 1969.

BOOKS BY ARTHUR MARDER

The Anatomy of British Sea Power, 1940.
Portrait of an Admiral, 1952. (Sir Herbert Richmond)
Fear God and Dread Nought, 3 volumes: 1952, 1956, 1959.
From the Dreadnought to Scapa Flow, 5 volumes: 1961, 1965, 1966, 1969, 1970.
From the Dardanelles to Oran, 1974.
Operation Menace, 1976.
Old Friends, New Enemies, 1981. Published posthumously.

About The Author

Born in Glasgow, Scotland, in 1909, Professor Geddes MacGregor was educated at the Universities of Edinburgh, Oxford, Paris, and Heidelberg. He is now Emeritus Distinguished Professor of Philosophy, University of Southern California, where he was also for some years Dean of the Graduate School of Religion. He has been married to his wife, Elizabeth, for more than 44 years; they reside in the Los Angeles area.

A naturalized citizen of the United States, Dr. MacGregor came to this country in 1949 as the first holder of the Rufus Jones Chair of Philosophy and Religion at Bryn Mawr—a position he held for eleven years before going to the University of Southern California.

He is the author of some 29 books, and of numerous articles. He has been Visiting Professor at many universities in the United States and Canada, including the University of Iowa and McGill. In 1967-68 he was Visiting Fellow at Yale; he was Canon Theologian at St. Paul's Cathedral, Los Angeles, from 1968 to 1974. He was Special Preacher at St. Paul's Cathedral, London, in 1969, at Westminster Abbey in 1970, several times at Princeton University Chapel, and in 1941 and 1985 at St. Giles' Cathedral, Edinburgh.

Geddes MacGregor has traveled widely in Asia, North Africa, and throughout Europe. He has given many lecture series in such cities as Montreal and Tokyo; and he holds awards and memberships too numerous to list here, though all may be found in *Who's Who In America* and in the British *Who's Who*.

Index